SEATTLE-TACOMA
and the
SOUTHERN SOUND

by Ronald R. Boyce

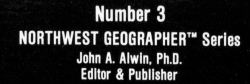

Number 3
NORTHWEST GEOGRAPHER™ Series
John A. Alwin, Ph.D.
Editor & Publisher

NORTHWEST GEOGRAPHER

John A. Alwin, Ph.D.
Editor & Publisher

Northwest Panorama Publishing, Inc.
Box 1858   Bozeman, MT 59771

Library of Congress Catalog Card Number: 86-062403

ISBN 0-9613787-2-7

Production Credits

Design and Layout: Ann Alwin, B.F.A.
Bozeman, Montana

Cartography: Chad Groth
Bozeman, Montana

Typesetting: Color World Printers
Bozeman, Montana

Printed in Japan by Dai Nippon Printing Co.,
Ltd., Tokyo

The Cover

Seattle-Bellevue area from 65,000 feet, about twice the cruising altitude of a commercial jet. A false color image, lush vegetation registers intense red, water appears blue and concrete and urbanized areas light green. Elliott Bay and the buildings of downtown Seattle can be seen on the left, a portion of Sea-Tac's runways at the bottom and Lake Sammamish on the right. Lake Washington and Mercer Island are in the center. From U.S. Geological Survey, EROS Data Center.

Title page

The city at work, view from the Harbor Island port area with the Seattle CBD aglow. Don Wilson, Port of Seattle photo.

Contents page

The everpresent Puget Sound sea gull. John Alwin photo.

About This Series

For its size, the Northwest is one of the world's most diverse regions. Few can rival its kaleidoscope of history, natural landscapes, climates, geology, urban centers, economic activity, and peoples. A geographer couldn't ask for a more interesting study area.

Each profusely illustrated and highly readable *Northwest Geographer*™ will focus on one component region or a specific Northwest topic. This captivating series is designed for the geographer in each of us and especially for the justifiably proud residents fortunate enough to call this special place home.

To be added to the *Northwest Geographer*™ Series mailing list and receive information on prepublication discounts on future books, write:

Northwest Panorama Publishing, Inc.
NORTHWEST GEOGRAPHER Series
P.O. Box 1858
Bozeman, MT 59771

SEATTLE-TACOMA AND THE SOUTHERN SOUND

By Ronald R. Boyce

Why did Seattle rise to its present prominence over other cities in Puget Sound? How does the past help us understand the region today? Why is the Puget Sound area growing so rapidly? What is truly distinctive about Seattle-Tacoma and sister cities on the Sound?

Ronald Boyce's latest urban expedition is calculated to capture the special character of Seattle and other cities on the Southern Sound. This one-of-a-kind book takes you back in time, lets you walk today's waterfronts, wonder at the rise of skyscrapers and explore the water world of the Sound.

Dr. Ronald R. Boyce is an urban geographer and Dean, School of Social and Behavioral Sciences at Seattle Pacific University. He is a long-time resident of Seattle and his wife, Norma, is a Tacoma native.

CONTENTS

The Place
An Introduction

In its summer splendor Puget Sound country looks like the best blend of colors from nature's palette. The emerald waters, deep and powerful, signify an inland sea, nestled between the white-peaked Olympics and the jagged Cascades. The rolling lowland topography, with its tree-green covering, blends with the blue beyond and creates a landscape fit for the cities it cradles.

To the outdoor-minded, the region is paradise. Spectacular vistas are so common it is almost impossible to find a house without a view. As one visitor put it, "aim your camera in any direction, close your eyes and shoot. You can't miss taking a great picture." In the distance the glacier-laden peaks stand ripe for the probing, snow-covered slopes invite skiing and wooded, winding trails exploring. Waters beckon the wanderer; there are salmon to be caught, life to be lived to its fullest in this pearl of nature that is Puget Sound.

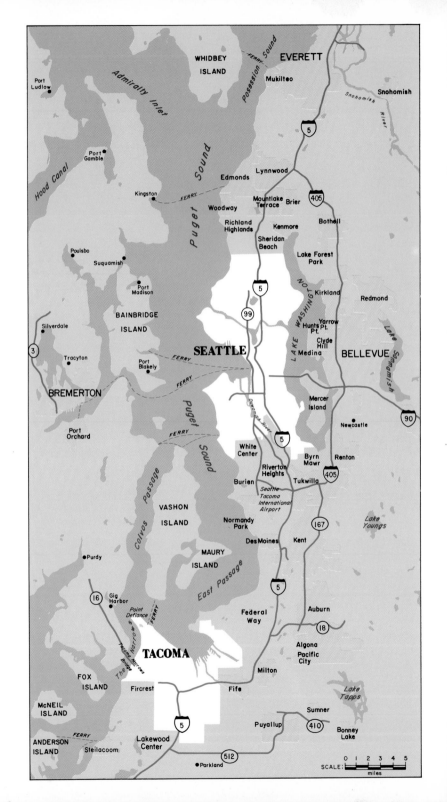

This is a land that at its best, especially in July and August, seems too good to be true. It is! During some of the winter months at Seattle's 47 degree north latitude, when short, dark and dripping days are the norm, even some natives have been known to mutter about Mother Nature. But most Sounders remain stubborn optimists, ignoring the weather and waiting for that first sunny day when the crocus announces the forthcoming promise of spring and the again glorious summer. While outsiders on those rare days may see slugs and sea-gull dung, and wince at the smell of rotting sea-weed, the natives remain serene. On such dark days they joke about the "magic mountain," claiming only the natives can see it, and use it as a weather barometer. "If you can see it, it's going to rain; if you can't, it's raining."

Perspectives on Puget Sound always have varied. The pioneering Denny Party of 1851 saw the Sound on a rainy November day from the low, wave-washed deck of the sailing ship, *Exact,* eight days out of Portland. As the newcomers peered over the rail through the misty, cold rain, some seasick, they squinted at the vaguely outlined tree-tipped shoreline. Although still hopeful, many were fast losing confidence in their decision to venture into the tall coastal timbers of the Northwest instead of the pleasant open valley of the Willamette.

Shorelands looked as if they were being squeezed flat by the heavy overcast. Sky and sea were almost together, leaving only a tiny sliver of shore. The overpowering impression was that of a thin strand of land spilling over with a great forest—trees down to the tops of the tide, trees reaching up every hill and rise till they blended with the bottom of overcast skies. Like an unwelcome wall, the trees stood straight and tall about the waters. Shores were blackish-grey, ominous, impenetrable. Only the sandy, tree-free spit at what the Indians called Smaquamox, today's Alki Beach of West Seattle, provided an open prairie-like area.

Waiting in a cabin still without a roof, his foot recently injured by a self-inflicted axe mishap,

At home high atop Seattle's Denny Regrade. Views are serious business in Seattle-Tacoma and their protection sometimes requires court action. Joel W. Rogers photo

5

Above: Heading into the Ballard Locks, a familiar passage for many of the one in eight Sounders who owns a boat.   Above right: Sound sentinel Mount Rainier rises above the clouds to greet air travellers on their final approach to Sea-Tac. Right: Early morning fog lifts from Hood Canal at the Madrona Private Homes near Union, revealing the Olympic Mountains beyond. John Alwin photos

and out of food because the skunks had eaten it, was David Denny, the advance scout. He had written the famous note to those who had weathered the Oregon Trail and were perched at Portland to ". . . come at once." His first words to the new arrivals, "I wish you hadn't come."

Later pioneers, crossing the Cascades by trail, followed the rivers to the Sound. Timber was the overpowering opportunity. All routes down the Cascades to the Sound were canyon-like corridors, tunnels between the timber—green gold waiting to be mined. Each mighty tree stood as an awe-inspiring invitation to wealth, a gift from God; not an obstacle to be cut down in order to get at the good earth, but a crop to harvest. Seemingly inexhaustible forests were wantonly leveled for profit. Soon lumber ships provided Californians with the stuff to build cities. Rail would offer avenues to the markets of the burgeoning Midwest.

Today most newcomers to the Sound arriving by air have a heavenly perspective fit for a hedonist. Mount Rainier appears off a wingtip—14,410 feet of upward volcanic thrust—ice-covered glory glistening in the sunshine. Like a serene and secure monument to the majesty of the region, the Mount Fujiyama of Seattle-Tacoma, it sits in stately quietness. The onlooker is reminded of Mount St. Helens, only recently erupted, and looks for stirring in the mighty nearby mountain.

Almost before one can recover from the sensation of being perhaps too close, a peek at the land below wisps by through a small streak in the clouds. Some ugly scars of timber clear-cuts bring a gasp of concern, but these are soon forgotten. A relatively flat, yet hilly, lake-laden land, lush with trees and interspersed with green, wet, soft grasslands suddenly is revealed. On the fringes of the urban complex asphalt roads appear, recently rain-washed, shining and free of traffic, then disappear up stream valleys or connect by curves one cozy isolated home to another. Outdoor-minded begin to dream of fishing the emerald lakes and

pristine streams, of hiking over distant hills or camping in one of the hidden valleys mapped out from the air.

Suddenly the distinctive triangular-shaped peninsula of Point Defiance and Tacoma comes into view. Adjacent is The Narrows, a turbulent conduit linking north and south Sound. The Narrows Bridge, a gigantic suspension structure, provides a monumental connection. And there is Tacoma fully occupying the Point, spilling southward and lapping around Commencement Bay, one of the best natural harbors in the world. A waterfront collection of unglamorous warehouses, belching smokestacks and geometric piers reminds visitors they are entering an urbanized area replete with industry, commerce and freeways, and packed with people. The landing gear lowers and the plane slows and drops in elevation on its final approach to Seattle-Tacoma International Airport (Sea-Tac).

On the right the flat fields of the Green River Valley contrast in function and form with the surrounding hill lands. These fields increasingly are being filled with sprawling warehouses, manufacturing plants and such burgeoning suburbs as Auburn and Kent. Yet even this close to touchdown, farmlands and open spaces are abundant. Residences pepper the hills. Even on the high country separating the Green River Valley from the Sound, houses look sheltered, sequestered among the trees.

In the distance is downtown Seattle. Its cluster of towering buildings, crowned by the massive Columbia Seafirst Center, overlooks Elliott Bay, making Seattle a city of such scenery as to cause even San Francisco to pale by comparison. The interspersion of Lakes Sammamish, Washington and Union inland from the Sound adds visual variety to this picture-book land, this sensory extravaganza—The Emerald City of Ecotopia.

Well over two million people are strategically implanted in discrete communities about the shores of the Southern Sound. Seattle, Tacoma, Bremerton, Everett and Olympia are among the primary nodes and ports. Dozens of other smaller places also profit from their water locations. Some are ferry terminals; some are military bases; some are marinas; others are simply charming places so situated as to take advantage of the water.

Seattle, the Emerald City, is also sometimes called the Queen City of King County. However, like central cities throughout the nation, it has been losing population. It reached its peak of almost 600,000 in the mid-1950s, but now claims less than 490,000.

Seattle is still gargantuan in comparison with her siblings and offspring on the Sound. Tacoma is home to approximately 160,000, Everett 56,000, Bremerton 35,000 and Olympia 27,000. The metropolitan area of Seattle approaches two million and that of greater Tacoma about 500,000.

Major port cities are backed up by inland communities. Some, such as Bellevue on the east side of Lake Washington, are sizable. With a population of about 80,000 and rapidly growing, it is Washington's fourth largest city. It contains a sparkling central high-rise business district; incredible Bell-Square, the smartest mall in the territory; and the greatest concentration of upper-income population in the state. Bellevue is surrounded by other affluent communities—Kirkland, Redmond, Issaquah and Renton, plus a host of high-income cities and towns that rim Lake Washington.

The silver strand of the wealthy is strung along the eastern shoreline of Lake Washington and around Mercer Island. Since World War II, bridges across the lake have provided easy access to and

9

from Seattle. Beginning near Interstate 90 on the southwestern edge of Bellevue and northward up the shore are the micro communities of macro prestige: Beaux Arts, Medina, Clyde Hill, Hunts Point, Yarrow Point and parts of Kirkland. Here along the Gold Coast are the $200,000-plus homes of the new wealthy elite, sheltered among the trees. These communities are backed by other high-income populations, with their smart shops, shopping centers, landscaped gas stations and the like, all of which have created for much of the East Side a Beverly Hills, Grosse Pointe environment.

Other communities have provided an almost complete infill along Interstate 5 between Seattle-Tacoma and Seattle-Everett. In these middle lands are some of the fastest growing places in the nation, including Lynnwood to the north and Federal Way to the south of Seattle. With the development of the Boeing 747 plant near Everett in the late 1960s and the anticipated Navy carrier base at Everett, the entire area from Mukilteo to Snohomish and Lake Stevens is vibrating with new growth expectations.

As even a highway map reveals, cities around the Sound comprise an interconnected supercity. This sprawling urban area from Puyallup to Tulalip, Shelton to Renton, and Bremerton to Bellevue and beyond, is rightfully called Pugetopolis. Towns and cities are located at choice sites and opportune places, at good harbors, at strategic highway crossroads and at amenity-laden spots within commuting range of Seattle and Tacoma. Today commuters crisscross the area via freeways, radios

Left: Gold Coast directory off the Evergreen Point Floating Bridge. John Alwin photo   Below: Portion of the Poverty Bay Quadrangle showing the rapidly growing Federal Way area. Purple-tinted areas show sections converted to urban land use between 1961 and 1981. Small black squares show individual houses. U.S. Geological Survey Map

tuned to live traffic reports keeping them up-to-date on conditions at the Southcenter Hill, the Renton S-curves and other problem stretches. Some commute southward from Marysville, north of Everett, to the industrial parks of the Green River Valley. Thousands make the daily trek across the Lake Washington floating bridges to downtown Seattle. Thousands more take the ferry trip from Vashon, Bremerton, Winslow, Kingston and Columbia and other West Sound towns and cities. Those in the Gig Harbor-Purdy corridor commute north to Bremerton or across the Tacoma Narrows Bridge to East Sound communities.

Puget Sound has changed roles as connector and divider of Pugetopolis. During the early days when water transportation was the only reasonable method of exporting the area's resources and

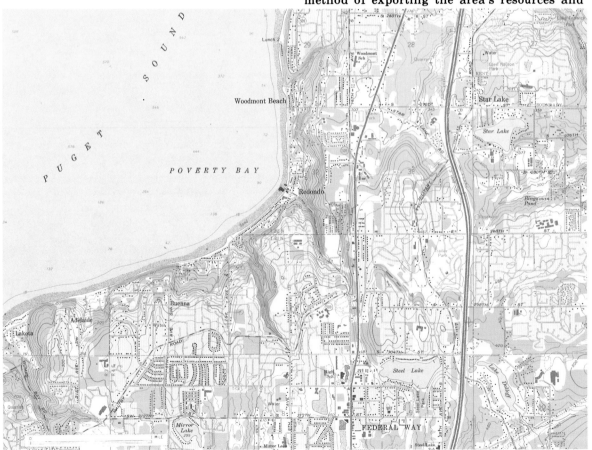

moving people about, the Sound acted as a great water highway for Seattle's celebrated Mosquito Fleet which connected east and west cities of the Sound in one intertwined whole. With the advent of railroads and later truck and auto transport, land became the paramount corridor of travel and the water was something in the way, to be bridged, ferried across or driven around.

Until recently urban growth has been elongated north and south along a narrow band on the eastern shorelands of the Sound and inland from Lake Washington. The hourglass shape of incorporated Seattle was extended to the entire area from Tacoma to Everett. The Sound became a great barrier, too broad to bridge and encumbered by slow-moving and expensive ferries.

In the '60s and '70s growth began moving upland and inland at an accelerated pace. Lake Washington was spanned in the early 1940s, again in the 1960s, and a third bridge is now under construction. Movement has surged eastward past Bellevue to the shores of Lake Sammamish. As growth circumscribes the lake, its terminal towns of Redmond and Issaquah are experiencing explosive growth. However, given the congestion and the distance, a counterbalance westward has been tipped. The westward communities on the other side of the Sound, despite the time and cost, are becoming more attractive than the far eastern communities. Bainbridge Island is booming. Many other West Side communities are becoming more desirable as they enter the gravitational grip of Greater Seattle.

Above right: So near and yet so far away, morning rush-hour commuting on I-5.   Right: Awaiting the arrival of the Tahlequah-Vashon Island Ferry at Tacoma's Point Defiance Ferry Landing. Ferries provide the only direct link to the outside for residents of quiet Vashon. John Alwin photos

Dairying on the Enumclaw plateau. Joel W. Rogers photo

FARMING IN THE URBAN SHADOW

Though overwhelmed by urban places and growing urban population, both Seattle's King and Tacoma's Pierce counties still have scattered pockets of picturesque, rural agricultural areas. Sprawl and suburbanization, however, continue to whittle away these productive farmlands. The problem is amplified by the fact that the more level and fertile valley bottoms with the greatest cropping potential also are in highest demand for development.

Economically 300 dairy farms and even more cattle raisers dominate agriculture in the Seattle-Tacoma urban shadow. In general, animal agriculture with its associated aromas and flies does not mix well with urban land uses. As subdivisions and country homes move in, surrounded dairies usually sell out. With notable exception, like the big Smith Brothers Dairy Farm outside Kent (the one with the giant Holstein statue), dairies and beef ranches tend to be in more outlying sections. In Pierce County, for example, dairy producers are most numerous around Roy and in the Buckley area. The lower Snoqualmie Valley domi-

nates King County's dairying industry and is home to the 1200-acre Carnation Research Farm near the town of Carnation.

Dairying in the Seattle-Tacoma fringe fits into the general western Washington dairy belt, the center of which is farther north outside Bellingham. An ability to operate in non-valley settings and a moist, mild climate in which pasture grasses thrive, make dairying an ideal type of agriculture for Western Washington. Its presence outside Seattle-Tacoma is consistent with associated dairying outside each of the nation's major population (market) centers.

Seattle and Tacoma near-urban areas also are noted for berry and vegetable production. Raspberries and strawberries are the number one and number two horticultural crops. Both berries thrive in the fertile river-bottom soils. As well as being marketed fresh locally, raspberries often are hand-picked in the cool, early morning hours, rushed to nearby Sea-Tac and flown to distant markets where they command a premium price.

Most locals are not aware of it, but the two-county area accounts for 90 percent of the nation's commercial rhubarb. It is produced both in the field and in hot houses, the latter method yielding the extra-red, highest grade variety. Lettuce (both head and leaf) and radishes are two other important local crops. For these, conditions are ideal enough that two crops a year are possible from the same field. The enticing berries and vegetables grown on the two counties' 10,000 acres of intensely cropped farmland greatly interest city folks. For over a decade the Puget Sound Farm Markets Association annually has distributed 100,000 free copies of a color map showing

Far left: Dan and wife Alice Campion moved onto their dairy farm outside Kent on their wedding day in 1935. Well into the Forties, they used horses in field work. Left: Now retired, Dan tends the apple cider machine. Below: The Campions retired their Twin Maples Dairy Farm in 1968 when they sold the 40-cow herd. Since then they have sold 60 acres to subdividers who are rapidly filling the fields with homes. John Alwin photos

where to buy produce directly from the farmers. Heading out to get fresh raspberries for preserves or strawberries to freeze for December shortcake is part of the seasonal cycle for many Seattle-Tacoma area residents.

At one time the Puyallup Valley outside Tacoma was an important producer of flower bulbs, especially daffodil, tulip and iris. Now more than a half-century tradition, the annual Daffodil Festival is still quite a celebration in Tacoma-Puyallup-Sumner-Orting. Despite the fact that each spring area growers send thousands of daffodils to decorate Johnny Carson's "Tonight Show" set, the industry has been in decline in the area for years with only a few producers left. Since 1945 the Puyallup Valley has lost

almost half its agricultural land, forcing out some growers and concentrating the industry farther north in the Skagit Valley/Mount Vernon area.

Concern for fast disappearing farmland in King County caused voters to pass the controversial King County Farmland Preservation Act in 1979. The idea was to use public funds to buy development rights to agricultural land. Farmers kept ownership of the land, but relinquished to the county rights to develop it. The per-acre compensation to the farmer was negotiated with the county, but generally was the difference between the value of the land if sold as farmland and the higher price it would bring if sold for development. By the end of the program in November 1985 the county had spent around $50 million on development rights for about one-fifth the county's farmland, or about 10,000 acres, most in the Green River and Snoqualmie River valleys.

Although now history, the Preservation Act remains controversial. Supporters point out that half the farmers who participated have indicated they would have sold their farms for development if not for the program. Critics say the county's purchase of development rights does not guarantee preservation of agricultural land, at best just assures future open space. Perhaps because of its controversial nature and procession of associated court cases, the citizens of Pierce County voted down a similar program in the 1980s.

If they desired, residents could be even closer timewise and thus their communities more competitive with those more inland. The speedy hydrofoil was offered on a trial basis to residents of Vashon Island. They turned it down. They were quite close enough to the hustle and bustle and commercialism of the big city, thank you.

The struggle for West Side communities in the coming decades may well be to maintain their peaceful, pristine and pleasant residential flavor with their winding roads, wooded areas and generally low population density. Meanwhile, the ferries are becoming larger. Jumbo Class superferries convey up to 2,000 passengers and 206 autos across the Sound at speeds up to 18 knots. As population booms, bridge possibilities again will be raised. The Sound has been bridged at the Tacoma Narrows and at Hood Canal. Smaller bridges have crossed stretches of the Sound, as at Deception Pass, Agate Pass and Port Washington.

Despite visionary efforts at regional cooperation through organizations including the Puget Sound Conference of Governments (PSCOG) and Municipality of Metro Seattle (METRO), there remains much rivalry among communities, even bitter jealousies, as between Seattle and Tacoma. Too often there is a spirit of non-cooperation, of general dissatisfaction between residents in the inner city and suburbia, and an outright paranoia on the part of big city mayors over any decentralization or the development of outlying areas.

The result is competition for what should be considered only within a general regional framework. For example, the Port of Seattle and the Port of Tacoma, much to the advantage of shipping companies and to the disadvantage of each other, vie for the same ocean traffic, each trying to make a better deal than the other, and in the process perhaps making both poorer. Most communities have adopted the attitude first articulated by Charles Wilson of General Motors that "what is good for General Motors is good for the country." Despite the obvious needs and benefits of cooperation, each community continues to plan its own destiny in rather splendid isolation, assuming its success will benefit all.

Seattle

The Emerald City's problems of growth are little compared to the problems of decline, something that ails both Seattle and Tacoma and many older central cities nationwide. Seattle is suffering from a population decline and aging facilities. Younger, more affluent and often white residents continue to move outward to suburban areas, leaving in their place the poor, the minorities and the elderly. Lately, however, social service personnel who deal with low-income residents in suburban areas have noticed an increase in the number of street people and other disadvantaged newly arrived from Seattle. Despite suburbanization, Seattle still is 80 percent white, quite a high percentage for an American central city in the 1980s. The city's Black and Asian components combine for a growing 17 percent of the population. In contrast, most Seattle suburbs are more than 90 percent white (Bellevue 93 percent, Lynnwood 93, Redmond 95, Kent 95, Kirkland 97, and Medina and Clyde Hill virtually 100 percent). Back in Seattle, were it not for the dramatic growth in the central business district and its major contribution to the tax base, the city would be in serious financial difficulty.

The outward expansion from the downtown area began when early Seattleites moved up the heights of First Hill, then along its spine to Capitol Hill. They continued to advance along Madison Avenue to the shores of Lake Washington. Others moved northwestward to Queen Anne Hill. By the turn of the century the city was hemmed in between the Sound on the west and Lake Washington on the east. It had no place to grow but north and south. The industrial and low-lying area was mostly to the south, so residential population primarily surged northward. The high-income areas jumped across Union Bay on the east and Salmon Bay on the west, and continued to advance up the coastlines of Lake Washington and Puget Sound. Middle-income population also moved northward across the Fremont Bridge, the Roosevelt Bridge and the Montlake Bridge.

Hills are generally oriented north-south, making major east-west roads from the Sound to Lake Washington a rarity. Most arterials run north-south, making east-west movement pitifully poor. Magnolia residents are closer to West Seattle, timewise, than to Lake City, or sometimes even the University district.

Tacoma

Old Tacoma is shaped like a triangle. At its northern apex is Point Defiance Park, the second largest municipal park of its type in the nation. On both sides downward from the point are majestic view properties overlooking The Narrows or Commencement Bay. On the east side of the triangle is the downtown area and the rapidly developing Port of Tacoma. The southwestern portion is truncated, claimed by Fircrest, Crystal Springs, Menlo Park and other comfortable suburban communities in unincorporated areas. Tacoma's growth largely has been limited to a southern land axis paralleling Interstate 5. Historically the main north-south spine was Pacific Avenue farther east, connecting Tacoma with Parkland.

Unlike Seattle, Tacoma has not been plagued by declining population with outmigration to suburbs out of annexation reach. But Tacoma's downtown has deteriorated dramatically. Despite considerable public moneys to reverse the retail decline, malls, escalades and public parking garages have been unable to curtail the exodus. Downtown Tacoma has been left without a single major department store since Peoples, the last holder-on, closed in 1984. Except for lunch hour, when office workers spill out to eat and shop, the downtown at times looks like the deserted set for a Hollywood movie. Walk/Don't Walk signals direct nonexistent pedestrians. The central business district's death knell for retailing was sounded in 1965 when the Tacoma Mall opened south of town along Interstate 5. Today about the only shopping crowd in downtown Tacoma is waiting at the bus stops for transit to the Tacoma Mall. The classy new Tacoma Financial Center, a spiffed-up Pantages Center and the impressive Sheraton Tacoma Hotel suggest rumblings of a downtown renaissance, at least as a financial service center, if not a retail mecca.

Above: The new Tacoma Narrows Bridge replaced its predecessor which blew down in 45-mile-per-hour winds in November 1940, just five months after its opening. Above right: Unloading containers at Sea-Land's new Tacoma terminal on the Sitcum Waterway. Right: For better or worse, peace and quiet abound in downtown Tacoma, even during the lunch hour. John Alwin photos

The Physical Realm

A reflection of the area's abundant precipitation, a Pioneer Square puddle. Joel W. Rogers photo

Many Sounders mistakenly assume that glaciers carved out the spacious lowland between the Olympics and Cascades. Glacial action explains the presence of Puget Sound and was important in producing many of the surface features we see today, but the lowland probably is best explained by a buckling downward of the underlying material with the rise of mountains to the east and west. This area still is forming geologically. Olympia's 1949 earthquake and a more recent one centered on Whidbey Island are reminders that nature is not yet finished forming the Sound.

The landscape legacy of earlier glacial activity is everywhere. Several times over the last 1.8 million years great glaciers moved southward out of Canada to fill the lowland. Recent studies of glacial deposits on Whidbey Island suggest about eight glacial periods. Ice last spilled into Puget Sound about 18,000 years ago. Upon reaching the Strait of Juan de Fuca it split, sending the Juan de Fuca Lobe westward up that strait and the Puget Lobe southward in the Sound. The Puget Lobe entered a lowland, but not one filled with an arm of the sea as today. Invaded was a broad, above sea level valley.

Radiocarbon dating of glacial deposits tells us that ice reached Seattle some time after 15,000 years ago. Ice pushed onward to its southernmost limit around Tenino, about 15 miles south of Olympia, about 14,000 years ago. At its maximum extent it filled the lowland and lapped high up onto the flanks of the Olympics and Cascades. The San Juan Islands were smothered. Bellingham lay buried under a mile of ice, the site of Seattle was covered by 3,000 feet, and the Tacoma area lay frozen under 1,800 feet of glacier. The lobe evidently did not linger long at its maximum and soon began melting back. By 11,000 years ago it had retreated across the United States-Canada border for the last time. Left behind were many of the land and water features we know today.

Action by the glacier helps explain the lowland's irregular surface and the obvious north-south grain. Ridges, lakes and arms of the Sound tend to parallel the direction of ice movement. In places the action of this and earlier glaciers and associated lakes was depositional, piling up gravel, sand and clay to depths of 3,000 feet. To the delight of view-lot addicts and the bane of town founders and civil engineers, hills made of material dropped and often streamlined and smoothed by the glacier were left as calling cards over wide areas, *a la* Seattle's Seven Hills (Queen Anne, Capitol, First, etc.). Had it not been made up of loosely consolidated material, the removal of Denny Hill would have been unfeasible.

Glacial scouring deepened basins that now are occupied by Lake Washington and Lake Sammamish. Ice scoured out and deepened what would become the Sound, making possible an invasion by sea water. In awesome testimony to its colossal size and weight, the Puget Lobe actually compressed the earth's underlying crust, thereby further lowering the Sound. Off Seattle the floor of the Sound now is as much as 840 feet below sea level, making it possible for large ocean-going merchant ships and the biggest of military vessels to ply these waters. Since the retreat of the heavy ice, the land has rebounded about 240 feet.

Puget Sound has a mild, marine west coast clime. Proximity to the Pacific Ocean usually means winters are not extremely cold nor summers excessively hot. The towering ramparts of the Cascades to the east normally are sufficient to block the extremes of heat and cold that hover in the markedly more seasonal Columbia Basin. Record temperatures at Seattle vary from a low of zero to a high of 100 degrees, but averages are much more agreeable. On a typical summer afternoon the mercury rises to a pleasant range of 70s to low 80s, with only high humidity detracting from the nearly ideal summer days. Nights predictably cool into the pleasant-sleeping 50s, making home air con-

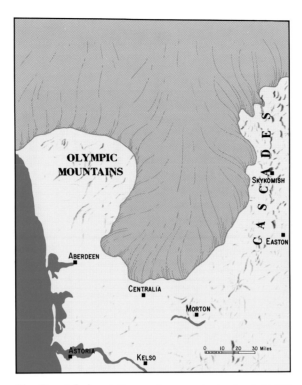

The Puget Lobe at its maximum extent, about 14,000 years ago. Source: H.E. Wright, Jr. and David Frey, eds, The Quaternary of the United States (Princeton: Princeton University Press, 1965), p. 343.

ditioning unnecessary. Mid-winter temperatures average in the 40s. According to a recent Rand McNally, *Places Rated Almanac,* Seattle-Tacoma and Bremerton have the mildest climates of all America's more than 300 metro areas, outside California.

With its classic maritime climate, Seattle on average experiences just three days a year when temperatures rise to 90° or higher and 31 days when the mercury drops to freezing or lower. Seasonal variation increases toward the south where the moderating effect of the Sound is reduced.

Nationally Seattle is not as well known for pleasant temperatures as it is for precipitation. Where else has an NBA game been postponed because of rain? (Actually a leaky roof at the Coliseum and rain combined to cause a wet court and cancellation of a Sonics game.) Surprisingly the

much maligned rainfall is less than in New York City, Philadelphia, Washington, D.C., Memphis and a long list of other American cities that do not have to fend off a dripping wet image. Like much of the Sound, Seattle-Tacoma lies within the rainshadow of the Olympic Mountains and averages 38 inches of precipitation annually.

Rainfall is even less to the immediate northeast of the Olympics in the heart of the rainshadow. Weather-wise Sounders know this is the area to head for to escape what at times seems endless drizzle. From Sequim to Anacortes and from the southern San Juans to southern Whidbey Island is a significantly less soggy corner of western Washington. Only 16 inches a year fall at Sequim, and Port Townsend's average 18 inches is less than Pullman's 20 on the dry side of the state. South of the rainshadow and separated from the Pacific and its moisture-laden storms by the Chehalis Gap, Olympia endures over 50 inches in an

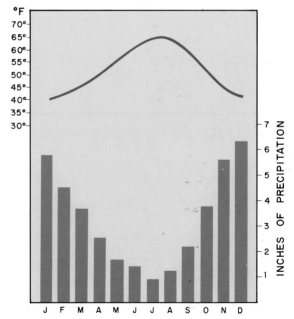

Climograph showing mean monthly precipitation and mean monthly temperatures at Sea-Tac Airport. Source: U.S. Dept. of Commerce, Local Climatological Data, Annual Summary with Comparative Data, Seattle-Tacoma Airport.

17

And this is just a youngster! The area's mild and moist climate and abundance of vegetation add up to ideal breeding grounds for slugs. So thick are these healthy gastropods at times that only the least squeamish residents venture barefoot into backyards after dark. John Alwin photo

average year. Even more precipitation falls on some of Seattle's East Side districts where air masses commence their climb over the west slope of the Cascades and begin purging themselves of moisture.

The problem for many in Pugetopolis is that the 30 to 50 inches of precipitation does not fall in heavy downpours so as to be over and done with, but comes in slow, microscopic, misty dribble. At Seattle it takes about 160 precipitation days to add up to 38 inches. Better than 75 percent of the yearly average falls from October 1 through March 31, taking six months to do what easily is accomplished in a matter of weeks elsewhere. Natives refer to this light rainfall, which does not require a raincoat or an umbrella and is not an acceptable excuse for not washing the car, as Oregon mist or California dew.

As predictable as the wet winter is the summer drought. At Seattle combined rainfall for July and August normally falls short of two inches. There have been Julys and Augusts with virtually no rain.

As any long-term resident can attest, not all precipitation falls as rain. Some occasionally has to be shoveled off walks. In fact, over the last 30 years, Seattle has averaged 15 inches of snow each winter. The more inland communities, including Bothell, Redmond and Issaquah are likely to receive even more snow than cities adjacent to the Sound. On snow-free mornings in Seattle it is easy to spot freeway commuters from the highest East Side locations by their snow-covered vehicles.

Throughout the region occurrence of snow is extremely variable, and often when it does fall it melts before accumulating measurable depth. Some years Seattle-Tacoma may get only a dusting, and several years may go by when a winter's total may add up to just a few inches of the white stuff. Just about when locals start to feel a bit smug about their lack of snow, and somewhat climatically superior to their cousins in Spokane, they are affronted by a major, national-news-caliber snowstorm.

The back-to-back storms of November 1985 that unleashed 17.4 inches on Seattle are just such an example. Accompanied by record-setting lows that dropped into the teens, area cities were virtually paralyzed. Schools closed for days. Commuting was a nightmare and scenic hills became dangerous slides. With a dearth of snow-removal equipment, sloping terrain and both cars and drivers unprepared for snowy roads, snow depths were more than sufficient to immobilize cities. Even veteran drivers from snowbelts quickly learn the realities of snow driving in the area when they attempt to drive up Seattle's Queen Anne Hill or take on Tacoma's Fairbanks Street or even South 11th in the heart of downtown! KIRO-TV meteorologist Harry Wappler reports that the number-one question among his justifiably concerned wintertime viewers is, "Is it going to snow?" One can only speculate how modern Seattle-Tacoma would cope with the 64 inches that fell in the record snowstorm of January 1880!

Above: Cross-country skiing moves to downtown following the back-to-back snowstorms of November 1985. Joel W. Rogers photo

Another disturbing climatic factor to gardeners and newcomers is lack of sunshine. For much of the year the standard forecast is an optimistic "partly sunny," not "partly cloudy" as is customary elsewhere. Trying to look on the meteorologic

Clouds almost always form and precipitation often develops. If conditions are right, with strong lifting, spring thunderstorms may result. Overcast and rainy conditions triggered by the convergence may be fairly localized. This explains why some sections of Seattle may be dismal and damp while the official condition at Sea-Tac is bright and sunny. To the dismay of residents, the convergence has been known to hang over Seattle for extended periods.

Natives know to take the weather as it comes. On good days they celebrate; they take off and take advantage of it. One cannot plan picnics and other outdoor events much in advance. On wet days locals ignore the weather and go about their accustomed routine. On misty days they venture out minus coats or umbrellas. Western Washingtonians say they rarely get "wet rain." Even so, there is the Washington patio, the Washington tennis court, the Washington sidewalk cafe—all covered.

In Pugetopolis a mild and moist climate creates an abundance of year-round greenery. Vegetation is terrarium-like with moss abundant, sometimes on all sides of trees, often forming deceiving patches of "grass" and decorating rooftops and sidewalks. Other vegetation, aside from the numerous coniferous trees, is almost sub-tropical appearing—even palm trees will grow. The old-growth forests in Discovery Park, Seattle's largest, and the virgin stands of towering Douglas fir, cedars and hemlock in 80-acre Weowna Park on Bellevue's east side are reminders of the majesty of the region's original vegetation.

Beneath the trees graceful ferns are prolific. Holly, ash, maple and birch abound. Flowering shrubs thrive and berry bushes are so ubiquitous a pantry full of preserves can be had from the bounty at the edges of a parking lot. Rhododendron grow wild and often reach ten or more feet in height. Left wild, vegetation becomes so dense it cannot be walked through without great difficulty. "Land Clearing" is a yellow pages listing.

bright side, this may be the place that coined the term "sun breaks." At Sea-Tac, the official area weather station, there are an average 228 cloudy, 80 partly cloudy and just 57 prized clear days a year. Winter and spring skies are predictably cloudy with, on average, a *total* of just 17 clear days between November 1 and April 30.

An abundance of cloudy, moist days is not surprising considering the area's maritime setting. In addition, a local phenomenon dubbed the Puget Sound Convergence zone boosts both cloudiness and precipitation. Thanks to professional TV meteorologists such as Harry Wappler, Jeff Renner and Steve Pool, who are as interested in education as forecasting, many Sounders know about this interesting occurrence.

The convergence most commonly occurs in the spring, just when locals are expecting clouds and

the drip-drip of winter to abate. It is linked to the prevailing northwesterly flow of air off the Pacific encountering the Olympic Mountains. Just like a giant rock in a stream of water, the highland deflects some of the airmass around its flanks. Air moves easterly through the Strait of Juan de Fuca, makes the bend around the northeast corner of the Olympic Peninsula and heads southward down the Puget Trough. To the south, air is deflected around the highland, through the low Chehalis Gap between the Olympics and Willapa Hills and then swings toward the north once into the southern Sound. Now on a collision course, the two air streams usually meet, or converge, between Seattle and Everett.

With nowhere else to go, the colliding air rises. As it ascends, it cools, losing its ability to hold moisture with each degree drop in temperature.

Settling the Southern Sound

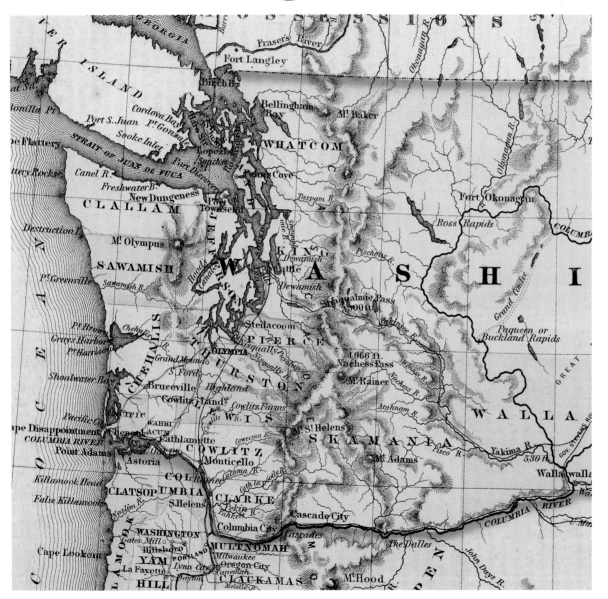

European ship captains had been examining the Sound for at least three quarters of a century before Seattle's founding. They surveyed the shorelands searching for gold, furs and trade with the Indians. They generally were unimpressed. There was no gold, there were few furs in comparison with areas farther north, and the Indians had little merchandise sought by Europeans. Forests abounded, but trees were not on the high-priority trading list.

Adventuresome Spanish were first to probe the area. In 1592 Juan de Fuca described the correct latitude for entrance to the Sound, but there is much myth in his presumed journey. On July 15, 1775, Bruno Hezeta splashed ashore just south of Point Grenville on what is now the Quinalt Indian Reservation and proclaimed the territory for Spain, thereby becoming the first European of record to set foot on the Northwest coast. The legendary Captain James Cook followed in 1778, naming Cape Flattery, but not entering the Strait of Juan de Fuca. In 1790 Samuel Quimper became the first European to sail well into the Strait and explore its islands, still known as the San Juans.

Englishman George Vancouver entered the elusive inland sea north of the Columbia River in 1792 and claimed all of Puget Sound for the infamous King George III. Although the monument commemorating his wading ashore from the *Discovery* is in Everett's Grand Avenue Park, he actually landed just to the north at Tulalip Bay and farther south at Mukilteo. Before sailing out of the Sound he named hundreds of landmarks, including Mount Baker, Vashon Island and Hood Canal. Vancouver named Puget Sound, the waters south of the Narrows at Tacoma, after Peter Puget, an

Puget Sound and beyond as it appears on the mid-1850s J.H. Colton atlas map. Courtesy of John Alwin

officer commanding one of the *Discovery's* small survey boats. Over time the name, Puget Sound, has been expanded geographically to include all the waters from Olympia to Bellingham and sometimes even the Strait of Juan de Fuca. Vancouver also named the mountain the Indians called Tacoma, Mount Rainier, in honor of Peter Rainier, a friend and fellow naval captain. Tacomans have tried several times to restore the original name to the mountain, even pursuing their cause in the hallowed halls of Congress, but to no avail.

English settlement began with the Hudson's Bay Company. Its Fort Nisqually became the Puget Sound area's first permanent white settlement in 1833 when built near the mouth of the Nisqually River south of today's Tacoma. The stockaded fur trade post quickly evolved into an important agricultural center with hundreds of nearby acres of crops overseen by the company's Puget Sound Agricultural Company.

In 1841 the American Lieutenant Charles Wilkes, on a scientific expedition, made detailed maps of Puget Sound and named numerous bays, passes and islands, including Seattle's Elliott Bay and Tacoma's Commencement Bay. Almost all members of his ships left their names indelibly imprinted on the Puget Sound seascape. Wilkes left very impressed with the navigational potential of the Sound.

American settlers first ventured into Puget country in mere dribbles (the fertile lands of the Willamette Valley offered greater agricultural potential). Tumwater, on the shore of the Southern Sound, was established in 1845. Following the 1846 Treaty of Oregon establishing the northern boundary of the United States at its present 49th parallel, settlement was encouraged by liberal land laws by which a married couple could easily acquire title to 640 acres. Lafayette Balch founded historic Steilacoom, Washington's oldest incorporated community in 1850, the same year Isaac Ebey and others settled on Whidbey Island. Port Townsend was founded about the same time. Elsewhere, isolated settlers began to stake out claims along the Nisqually, the Puyallup, the Duwamish and in other fertile bottomlands, and even atop Seattle's Beacon Hill.

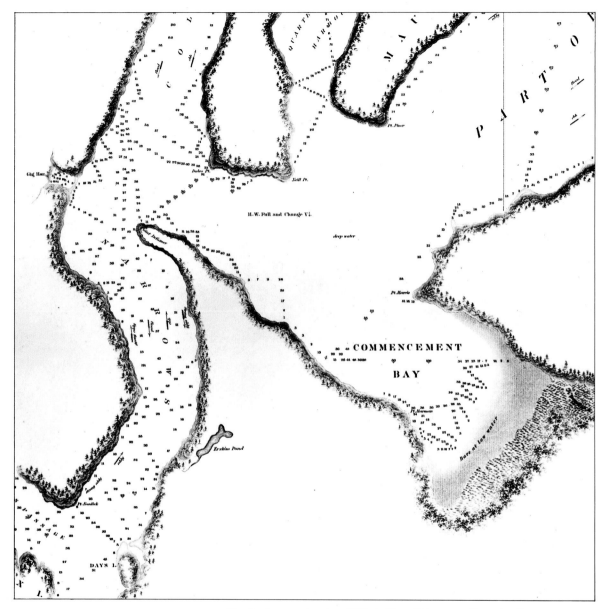

Nautical map showing Wilke's Expedition soundings in Commencement Bay, The Narrows and adjacent waters. From United States Exploring Expedition, During the Years 1838, 1839, 1840, 1841, 1842 Under the Command of Charles Wilkes, U.S.N., *Atlas of Charts, Vol. II (Philadelphia: C. Sherman & Sons 1858), p. 87.*

"Puget Sound & Mt. Rainier from Whitby's [sic] Island," a John Mix Stanley lithograph from the federal government's 1850s Northern Railroad Survey.

So on that rainy 13th of November, 1851, when the *Exact* dropped its 22 wet and weary passengers at Alki Point, pioneers and settlements already had taken root in the region.

After seeing the fertile lowland of the Duwamish as part of an advance scouting party, David Denny sent back to Portland his famous note to brother Arthur, reporting, "We have examined the valley of the Duwamish river and find it a fine country. There is plenty of room for one thousand settlers. Come at once." It would appear that he was thinking more about farming than about lumbering or city-building. There is much debate about those intentions. At any rate, the Duwamish was bypassed by the Denny party. The Lows and Terrys laid out their "New York" at Alki, and the Bells, Borens and Dennys homesteaded land on the eastern shores of Elliott Bay. They were joined in 1852 by community-minded Doc Maynard, a close friend of Chief Seattle. That same year Henry Yesler arrived and set up a lumber mill. Aboriginal settlers moved aside and made room for their new neighbors.

The main invasion of settlers to the Sound began in 1853-54 when timber seekers came to set up mills. These entrepreneurs, many from Maine and with considerable wealth and logging experience, set about supplying logs to a booming California market. Among these earliest mill towns were Port Townsend, Port Gamble, Port Ludlow, Port Madison and Port Blakely. Bainbridge Island and the northern part of Kitsap Peninsula and the Hood Canal area were soon a seething hotbed of milling activity. Settlers nearby, especially those at Coupeville on Whidbey Island, thought they surely would become the major metropolis of the Sound, given their protected port, northerly location on the Sound and extensive agriculture and logging activities.

By the late 1850s numerous sawmills were scattered about the Sound. Most were one-company mill towns. Pope & Talbot's Port Gamble was one of the largest. However, the distinction of having the first steam-powered sawmill went to the enterprising Henry Yesler of Seattle, the city's first industrialist.

Much has been written in local lore about the motives and insights of the founding Denny party in choosing the Puget Sound and the Seattle sites over the Willamette Valley and Portland. The standard explanation is that these were settlers primarily more interested in city-building and commerce than in tilling the soil. Some even endow these pioneers with mystic vision, beginning in Illinois, for founding a great city on Puget Sound. Still others, writing about their ancestors, claim they were harder-working and perhaps brighter than their neighbors.

Neither Puget soil nor climate is of much value for farming. Land suitable for agriculture is extremely limited. Farming is only feasible on the alluvial soils of river valleys, and only then for crops not requiring great amounts of sun. More-over, the demands for timber from California were so great and rewards for selling it so lucrative, that few other economic endeavors seemed reasonable.

Members of the Denny party hardly had time to settle in before their group was solicited for logs. The *Leonesa* was on its way to Olympia in a frantic search for logs for San Francisco. Not having an established source, the captain rowed ashore at Alki and asked the new settlers if they could supply him with timber. The settlers agreed and signed a contract, but found logs difficult to get at Alki. Some began thinking about better sites with more ready access to timber and suitable docking areas.

In February 1852, after a rather crude depth sounding of the Elliott Bay shorelands using a clothesline and some horseshoes, the Bells, Borens and Dennys laid out claims on the east shore of Elliott Bay, in dense trees and adjacent to deep water. Terry and Low already had laid claims at

Left to right above: Seattle founders Arthur Denny, David Denny, Dr. David "Doc" Maynard and Henry Yesler. Museum of History & Industry, Seattle, WA photos
Right: On the edge of the wilderness, Seattle, 1860. Yesler's house in foreground sits on the corner of what is now First Avenue and James Street in today's Pioneer Square Historic District. Special Collections Division, University of Washington Libraries, Prosch photo, Neg. No. 2244

An 1882 bird's-eye view shows a Seattle creeping up the still-forested hillsides. Crossing a now in-filled section of Elliott Bay, a Columbia and Puget Sound Railroad Company train returns to the King County coal fields after delivering a load to the coal docks.
Museum of History & Industry, Seattle, WA photo

Alki before the main party arrived. This tiny east shore settlement initially was called Duwamps, but the name soon was changed, evidently at Doc Maynard's suggestion, to Seattle, namesake of the friendly chief whose Indian name was Sealth.

Claims were platted into city streets and blocks in a most irregular pattern, not oriented one with another and with total disregard of the topography. The scrambled street pattern is one of the legacies left by the pioneers—a system comprised of several different orientations, still causing great inefficiencies and confusion. Pie-shaped pieces of no-man's land remained between the differently oriented plats.

Trade was critical during the first year, with logs providing the money necessary to buy supplies from San Francisco. The log business was highly lucrative for all concerned. Salmon were so numerous that fishing was another natural resource ripe for exploitation.

A decade or so after its founding, with barely 200 residents, few would have given Seattle the edge over other towns to become the paramount place of Puget Sound. Olympia and Steilacoom were larger, and Olympia was the capital and provided the best route to the interior. It was also closest to Portland, the expected, and first, railroad connection.

Port Townsend, Port Blakely and other sawmill centers were growing rapidly and had other advantages. They were better backed financially and had locational superiority to California markets. They were closest to the ocean and on the preferred west side.

Unlike Portland with its Columbia, Seattle was not near the mouth of a great river and the natural focus of a vast, natural tributary area inland. No dominant rivers empty into the Sound. Rivers on the east side run largely parallel to each other, are not navigable for large vessels without extensive dredging and commonly terminate in tidal deltas.

Between Seattle's Elliott Bay and Commencement Bay in Tacoma, Commencement Bay is the better natural harbor. Much was said about the splendor of Commencement Bay, but few had accolades about its northern neighbor. Wilkes certainly was unimpressed. Upon seeing Elliott Bay in 1841 he wrote, "The anchorage is of comparatively small extent, owing to the great depth of water as well as the extensive mud flats; these are exposed at low water. Three small streams enter the head of the bay, where good water may be obtained. I do not consider the bay a desirable anchorage: from the west it is exposed to the prevailing winds, and during their strength there is a heavy sea."

Had Lake Union and Lake Washington been navigable from the Sound, Ballard, on Salmon Bay, might have become the kingpin settlement of the eastern Sound. However, with no connection until completion of the Lake Washington Ship

Canal in 1917, these lakes acted as barriers, not avenues, to eastward penetration. Certainly Seattle had no special advantages in terms of inland access.

After extensive surveys that began in the early 1850s, several sites emerged as the possible terminal for a transcontinental railroad—Olympia, Steilacoom, Tacoma, Seattle, Mukilteo and Port Townsend. As the long-awaited 1873 decision date approached, it was assumed the three finalists were Commencement Bay at Tacoma, Elliott Bay at Seattle and Port Gardner Bay at Mukilteo. The choice finally came down to Seattle or Tacoma, with those in Seattle certain they would prevail. Businessmen in Seattle offered the railroad city lots, acres of developed land nearby, waterfront property, cash and other concessions all totaled worth hundreds of thousands of dollars. Tiny Tacoma appeared to offer little by comparison. It was with great surprise and despair to Seattleites when, on July 14, 1873, the Northern Pacific Railroad wired those resounding words to Arthur Denny in Seattle, "We have located the terminus on Commencement Bay."

Above: Tacoma, 1871, then a mere village on the shore of Commencement Bay. Two years later it was announced the town had been selected terminus for the Northern Pacific Railroad. Washington State Historical Society, Tacoma, WA photo   Left: Tacoma's Pacific Avenue from 12th Street, 1887. Washington State Historical Society, Tacoma, WA photo

Bainbridge Island's Port Blakely, circa 1890. Washington State Historical Society, Tacoma, WA photo

Seattle's designs on dominance of the Sound seemed dashed that summer of '73. Its future prospects were suddenly overshadowed by Tacoma, a two-year-old upstart village 30 miles to the south, with only a tenth the 2,000 residents of Seattle. Several businessmen thought the future of Seattle hopeless and moved to Tacoma. It had the backing of the first railroad destined to serve the Sound; it had a magnificent harbor and, nearby, the highly productive agricultural Puyallup River Valley. With its selection as rail terminus, Tacoma's competitive advantage over its sister cities on the Sound seemed assured. Tacoma appeared destined to become the foremost city on the Sound and worthy of its "City of Destiny" title.

Sensing that *this* was the community with a future, Weyerhauser Timber Company, the largest owner of forestland in Washington, soon chose Tacoma for its headquarters. However, because of fiscal problems, the Northern Pacific folded and was taken over by new investors. The new company president was more favorably disposed toward Portland than either Seattle or Tacoma. Due to delays the railroad did not reach Tacoma until 1883, and then via Portland. Finally in 1888, fifteen years after first announced, it crossed the Cascades through Stampede Pass and terminated at Tacoma.

The delay of the railroads proved to have a positive side for Seattle. It prevented the city from becoming an overly specialized port in timber or sawmilling. Seattle also was protected from the high-handed tactics of the railroad companies. Residents concentrated, instead, on making the city a general trading emporium, one of the few options available.

Yet Seattle had something no other settlement could offer or capture—a central, gateway location on the Sound. Being centrally situated, vessels from Seattle could be dispatched equally easily to Olympia or Port Townsend. Regular runs of passengers and supply vessels enabled Seattle to gain a supremacy on inland Sound traffic.

With Seattle neither a company town nor a railroad town, it early established a diverse manufacturing and trading line—timber and lumber, fishing and canneries, coal and bunkering and especially, transportation. It was a logical place of assembly and distribution for the various Sound towns. The group of vessels that maintained this linkage eventually was known as the Mosquito Fleet, because the small, non-ocean-going craft flitted about among the various ports, tying them all to Seattle.

Water links inland with Lake Washington also seemed to offer economic potential. In 1853 a federal government survey party suggested a waterway linking Puget Sound and the lake. It was to foster commercial growth of tiny Seattle and provide a safe harbor for American warships. Large-

26

X1040

Left: View down Rainier Vista at Seattle's 1909 Alaska-Yukon-Pacific Exposition from the U.S. Government Building. Built on a site borrowed from the University of Washington campus, the layout of the Exposition is mirrored today in the geometry of the central campus. The Arctic Circle fountain in the center of the photo is now called Drumheller Fountain. Museum of History & Industry, Seattle, WA photo   Below: Supplies for Klondike-bound miners overflow onto the sidewalk at the Cooper and Levy store on First Avenue South in downtown Seattle. Sled dogs in training prior to Klondike duty. Museum of History & Industry, Seattle, WA photo

scale commercial coal mining near Renton in the 1870s added fuel to talk of an interior water link. Even with poor transport the export value of coal shipped from Seattle exceeded lumber by 1881. Two general schemes surfaced, a northern and a southern canal. The latter would have seen a five-mile-long channel dug from the Duwamish, running north of Beacon Hill and through Rainier Valley to the lake. The winning plan called for a canal linking the Sound and lake via Shilshole Bay, and was completed in 1917 as the Lake Washington Ship Canal.

In 1893 Seattle was chosen as the terminus of the Great Eastern Steamship Company, establishing regular trade services with the Orient. The Japa-nese Steamship Company, the Nippon Yusen Kaisha, also selected Seattle as terminus, choosing it over San Diego or other cities of Puget Sound. On August 31, 1896, when the first major shipments of silk and tea arrived, Seattle declared a legal holiday.

Seattle also promoted very early trade with Alaska. This commerce, like the Mosquito Fleet operations, was considered rather insignificant by those in other Sound ports. However, when the Klondike Gold Rush began in 1897 and that ship with the mystical "ton of gold" arrived, Seattle was in an enviable position to take advantage of its established Alaskan links and the promising Gold Rush trade.

1906 penny postcard view of scenic Tacoma. Card caption identifies mountain as "Mt. Tacoma." Courtesy of Alison Alwin

It was Erastus Brainard, a former newspaperman then employed by the Seattle Chamber of Commerce, who sewed up the Seattle-Alaska connection. He undertook one of the most effective media blitzes ever conceived. His main message was that people had to come to Seattle in order to outfit themselves for the Klondike. He encouraged Seattleites to write relatives and their former hometown papers touting Seattle and the Gold Rush. One of Brainard's techniques was to write to mayors in large cities asking whether any of their citizens had contracted Klondike Fever, then suggested that coming to Seattle was the only cure. It worked magnificently and he published the mayoral replies as news items.

Seattleites today are so affronted by his crass promotionalism that most authors discount Brainard's efforts. Tacomans, however, think Brainard was the epitome of the Seattle Spirit—much fluff, puff and bluff and loaded with ridiculous exaggeration of claims. Nonetheless, Brainard clearly was responsible for gaining the assay office for Seattle, of key importance in the Alaskan gold trade. He also made certain that everyone everywhere was aware of a little place called Seattle on Puget Sound. For those who may have missed the message, the 1909 Alaska-Yukon-Pacific Exposition focused national attention on Seattle and its growing role as portal to Alaska and the entire Pacific Basin.

Another key factor in Seattle's success over other communities was the convergence of commerce-building railroads. With lines radiating outward in all directions but the west by the turn of the century, Seattle became the Chicago of the Sound. Innovative civic actions, particularly at the beginning of the twentieth century, kept the railroads from dominating the affairs of the city. It soon was apparent that as well as having the best water links, Seattle had a decided land transportation advantage over other Sound cities and was on its way to becoming the largest on the Sound.

The supremacy of Seattle by the beginning of this century was not necessarily sufficient to assure its continued prominence. Certainly without new successes, Seattle today would be only somewhat larger than Tacoma. Most of the early milltowns faded fast as would-be city contenders. By 1910 most were in marked decline, having some historical significance and, of course, considerable Puget charm, but of limited value as feeder settlements for Seattle.

In addition to its historic role as hub for water and land transport, the success of Seattle has resulted from four main factors: 1) the military presence, including base building, shipbuilding and more in and around Seattle, 2) the continued trade, largely in-transit, with Alaska and the Orient, 3) the rise of Boeing (often called "Boeings" by locals), and 4) offspins relating to Seattle's status as regional capital of the Northwest, perhaps more of an effect of the first three than a cause for initial growth.

The greatest stimulators and producers of growth in Seattle and Puget Sound have been war-related. In 1891 the Sinclair Inlet town of Bremerton was chosen over other places on the West Coast as site for a major military facility, the Puget Sound Naval Shipyard. In 1897 Camp Lawton on Magnolia Hill (now a city park) was established in Seattle. Even the Spanish-American War was beneficial to Puget Sound. Massive concrete bunkers and military operations were installed in 1898 at Camps Worden, Casey and Flagler. Each fort was located on a point of an imaginary equilateral triangle so as to provide crossfire coverage of Admiralty Inlet, the entrance to the Sound. World War I brought Tacoma its sprawling, nearby Fort

First Hill from King Street Station, Seattle, Wn.

1908 penny postcard view of Seattle's First Hill from King Street Station. Courtesy of Robert Alwin

Lewis. It was also during the First World War that Keyport, near Poulsbo, was chosen as a Navy torpedo testing station, today's Naval Underseas Warfare Engineering Station. And during World Wars I and II, major shipbuilding activity occurred at Seattle, Tacoma, Bremerton and other places on the Sound.

Today McChord Air Force Base, Fort Lewis and Madigan General Army Hospital are major contributors to the economic base of Tacoma and the region. Naval Submarine Base Bangor, the first home for the nation's Trident submarines, became operational north of Bremerton in 1981. The Navy is planning a major installation at Everett. Other military operations, such as Sand Point Naval Air Station, several Naval reservations and Coast Guard installations are additional economic pluses for the region.

Since its inception in the 1890s, trade with the Orient and with Alaska has taken on various forms. Exports included timber and fish, and agri-cultural products mainly from east of the Cascades, and imports were primarily destined for places in the Midwest and beyond. Seattle, therefore, has long been mostly an in-transit port, providing only a minimum market. The early silk ships swiftly unloaded their cargo on Seattle docks to be hustled on special silk trains heading to New England mills. It was the China-Japan silk trade that gave Seattle considerable impetus in the 1920s during the post-World War I economic doldrums.

Boeing is another key to Seattle's success. Although riding a roller-coaster employment course since its inception, Boeing has been outstanding in both military and domestic commercial endeavors. Its rise to glory, however, rests entirely on military orders during World War II when the famous "B bombers" were selected as our and the Allies' heavy-duty planes. This one company with its dozens of facilities in greater Seattle, Renton, Kent and Everett, since World War II has provided local employment for from 40,000 to more than 90,000.

Other sectors of the general economy are larger than Boeing, but one must remember that Boeing is but a single company. Tourism is sizable, but seasonal. Seattle's first major promotional thrust was with the World's Fair in 1962. The multi-faceted Seattle Center and its Space Needle remain major tourist draws. Timber and fishing are of decreasing importance.

Finally, Seattle's importance is shown in its status as a regional capital and focus for the nation's Northwest corner. Seattle continues to act as interchange center among other cities, but instead of shuttle services among cities of the Southern Sound, it now provides interconnections for a vast hinterland stretching into central Montana. Sea-Tac is the undisputed hub and gateway airport for the entire Northwest.

As a regional capital Seattle claims the major medical centers, the headquarters of banks, insurance and other companies, and the sites for all manner of manufacturing firms geared to serving a large regional market. It is home to the University of Washington, one of the nation's premier institutions of higher education. The Emerald City stands out for its excellence in the fine and performing arts. And loyal fans of the Seahawks, Sonics and Mariners are thick throughout a multi-state area. The most impressive skyline of any city west of Chicago is undeniable evidence of Seattle's supremacy within the nation's northwest quarter. Recent completion of a crowning cathedral of commerce, the 943-foot, 76-story Columbia Seafirst Center, the tallest skyscraper west of Chicago and north of Texas, is a fitting exclamation mark.

Peoples of Puget Sound

The first people arrived on the Sound from the north more than 10,000 years ago and witnessed at least the melting back and final withdrawal of the Puget Lobe. These first Washingtonians entered a rich region where life was relatively easy. They developed social systems and economies quite distinct from those in other harsher, neighboring environments.

Indians north of Vancouver Island, such as the Haidas, have been popular study targets for anthropologists. These vigorous tribes were skilled in warfare, made magnificent wood carvings, tall totem poles, massive dugout canoes and even had whale-hunting skills. They were superior militarily to the Sound tribes, and raided them periodically in their great war canoes in order to take women and children as slaves.

Likewise, the Indians on the inland plateaus to the east or farther south were rich in artifacts and skills. These Indians also made pottery, wove beautiful multi-colored blankets and crafted fine jewelry. Those inland were great hunters, had horses by the 1700s and were tall and handsome.

In contrast, the Coast Salish of the salt water Sound were much less appreciated and interesting to the explorers, traders and settlers. The Indians here wore almost no clothes or shoes and tended to be short and stocky. They sometimes rubbed themselves with foul-smelling oil of the dogfish and lived in what appeared to be makeshift, vermin-infested settlements. Women did most of the work, while men seemed to languish lazily about camp.

On Skokomish River near Hood Canal, two Salish women in rain gear pose in front of a traditional cattail reed, or mat, house, circa 1912. Special Collections Division, University of Washington Libraries, Edward Curtis photo, Neg. No. NA231

The Siwash

Aside from casual explorer vessels, fur traders were the first Europeans to impact Sound Indians. It is claimed by some that the Indian word the Salish called themselves, Siwash, is actually a corruption of the French-accented English word, savage.

Through contacts with traders and with Catholic missionaries and priests, most Indians had been exposed to Christianity by the time American settlers arrived. However, the missionaries carried considerable cultural baggage, which generally confused the Indians. First, they despised the natives' nakedness and promptly set out to dress them properly. They also objected to many of their social customs. The potato was introduced and generally adapted, but farming was not something the Indians needed or desired. In terms of spiritual conversion, many were baptized and accepted Catholicism, like Chief Seattle, but in their hearts they remained unadulterated animists.

Each village and tribe had its own illahee or territory for fishing, gathering of berries and bulbs and for other purposes. A water-oriented people, Indians avoided the dense forest, and located instead on rivers and along the shores of the Sound. Often the illahee extended for considerable distances in a kind of leapfrog and spotted pattern about the rivers. Villagers moved regularly with the seasons. During the spring and summer they lived in temporary camps while fishing and gathering berries and bulbs. Some of each was preserved for winter. During winter months they lived in a more substantial camp, with longhouses made of cedar boards, along a river bank or shoreline where clams and fish were abundant.

The relative isolation of one tribe from another led to separate subdialects and slightly different customs. Even so, potlatches and intermarriages were held among tribes, and there were periodic gatherings of tribal chiefs.

The climate was so mild, fish so plentiful, and bulbs, berries, roots and other plants so abundant, that the Salish did not have to develop great skill or work very hard in order to survive. Salmon are no doubt the easiest of all fish to catch, returning by the thousands to the small streams to spawn. All that was necessary to catch them during this time were sharp sticks, crude weirs or nets. On the beaches clams were ready for easy digging. Berries and roots from the wild onion, carrot or camas (which was made into flour) were found in prairie-like clearings near rivers. Cedar bark was perfect for clothes-making and the weaving of clam baskets, as well as their distinctive waterproof, pointed bowl hats. About the only environmental tending was women burning trees to retain meadows, something that later perturbed loggers.

Sound Indians had one skill greatly valued by the early settlers—the making of dugout canoes. These were slowly hacked out of large fallen cedar trees using hot rocks, fire, water and crude scraping instruments. This skill was limited to the Indian elders who had the requisite patience and ability.

Siwash canoe being constructed from cedar log, Coupeville, Whidbey Island, 1902. Special Collections Division, University of Washington Libraries, O.S. Van Olinda photo, Neg. No. NA824

Until the arrival of settlers, Indians could operate much in their accustomed manner. With white settlement, however, conflict was inevitable. Sites Indians considered their own were the very places homesteaders wanted—flat meadowlands upriver. Neither group cared much about the uplands and places appreciably distant from water.

Had the Indians been hill or mountain dwellers, conflict might have been delayed for decades but, in fact, the worst possible scenario was created, a classic conflict of cultures. Whites neither appreciated the Indian culture nor understood its economy. Indians, likewise, found the customs of the whites, particularly as pertained to land ownership and commercial activities, absolutely alien and unacceptable.

The "solution" was swift but short-sighted—place the Indians on reservations. Even a cursory understanding of the general Indian patterns of livelihood would have revealed inadequacies in this supposed solution. Indians from different tribes, often having little in common, were allocated the same reservation. By 1855 Indians had signed the white man's treaties, prepared in advance for their "X." About a half dozen Indian reservations were created around the Sound. Initially these were only about a thousand acres each, but within a few years most were greatly increased in size. Even so, they were far too small for Indians to survive in their accustomed manner. Their primary fishing and gathering spots on the rivers and bays were off the reservations and off-limits, newly claimed by white settlers.

The end result was that the Indians of Puget Sound, like elsewhere on the American frontier, were devastated by disease, alcohol and reservation life. In fact, the number of Puget Sound Indians had been greatly reduced by measles, smallpox and syphilis decades before permanent settlers arrived.

Nevertheless, a few Indians adjusted well to the white man's world. Some became highly regarded workers in the mills, obtaining leadership positions. Others pursued advanced education and acculturated to such an extent that their Indian identities and heritage disappeared. Stripped of their culture and aliens in their own country, the general body of Indians understandably had problems adjusting to the new order.

Today Native Americans are one ethnic group generally not content with the new social and economic environment. Recently they have become more vocal. They have won several important cases that recognize their integrity as separate nations, establish certain privileges (liquor, gambling and fireworks) on Indian reservations and have upheld treaty promises in which they have been guaranteed access to fish and wildlife. The battle is by no means over.

Problems pertaining to Native Americans also extend to the reservations and their internal management. The Puget Sound area's Indian reservations include more than 81,000 acres of land. Some, like the Puyallup (17,900 acres), the Tulalip (22,490) and the Port Madison (7,284) are sizable. Today there are 11,000 tribal members, of which about 6,400 reside on the reservations.

Conflicts have arisen on at least two fronts—the shrinking ownership of the Indian-owned reservations and the increasing percentage of resident non-Indian population. Over time, Indians on area reservations have sold their lands to non-Indians, and today, on average, only five percent of a reservation's land is Indian-owned.

The Puyallup Indian Reservation is a good example. This large reserve has dwindled in Indian ownership to just 90 acres, or less than one-half of one percent of the original reservation land. Almost 97 percent of the population is non-Indian. With fewer than 900 members of the Puyallup tribe at home on their own reservation, the Puyallup's claim to thousands of acres of Milton, Fife and Tacoma, including a portion of the Port of Tacoma on Commencement Bay, has been one topic of conversation that has outranked the weather.

When Washington's hop production was centered in the Puyallup Valley, Indians provided much of the hand labor necessary for harvest. Special Collections Division, University of Washington Libraries, Edward Curtis photo, Neg. No. 292

The Newcomers

The consequence of the occupancy system was that new settlers penetrated every available river valley. In doing so, they wiped out almost all vestiges of Indian names. Some remain, such as Puyallup and Mukilteo, but most on today's highway maps are contrived, having no historic Indian basis. Instead, towns generally were named from two sources: the names of the pioneers, which was most common, or their former hometowns or areas. Hometowns included Bellevue (after Bellevue, Indiana) and Clyde Hill (after the Clyde River of Scotland). An interesting exception is Kent, named in 1890 after a then famous hop-growing county in England. Usually settlements went through several name changes, the later settlers erasing the name of earlier pioneers.

Tacoma is known for its rich ethnic mix. Here an Italian vendor, probably on Commerce Street, offers his wares, circa 1905. Tacoma Public Library photo

The primary inland penetration from the Seattle settlement was up the Duwamish and its two main tributaries, the White (later renamed Green River) and the Black River. By the mid-1850s, the entire flood plain of the Duwamish and its tributaries was occupied. Georgetown, on the Duwamish, was settled well before Seattle. Kent (then called White River and later Titusville), Auburn, Enumclaw up the river valley, and Renton at the headwaters of the Black River were settled in 1853. All these early settlements were characterized by logging, lumbering, chicken and egg raising and general vegetable production geared to the nearby Seattle market.

Coal was the primary motive for development in southeast King County. First discovered when land was being cleared for settlement in Renton, major mines were developed at Newcastle and in the Maple Valley area, especially at Black Diamond, which became the county's largest coal producer. Miners worked to a depth of 6,200 feet, reputedly lower than any other mine in the country. The mines have long been closed, but the towering slag heaps and neat rows of company houses are reminders of when coal was king.

During the 1880s the entire Southern Sound boomed. Railroads were constructed, allowing many valleys to be more closely tied to Seattle. And suitable river valleys were brimming with hops. When a devastating blight ruined hop crops in Europe, Western Washington became, for a decade or so, hop center of the world. Both Chinese and Indians were heavily employed in harvesting. Because of the Panic of 1893, the restoration of hop production in Europe and, especially, the problems of disease infestation and blight in Western Washington, hop production here ceased abruptly, taking root in the Yakima Valley on the other side of the Cascades.

Lake settlements, including Woodinville, Juanita and especially Kirkland had high expectations. In 1888 the Moss Bay Iron and Steel Company of America was organized with plans to make Kirkland the Pittsburgh of the West. Peter Kirk, an English iron and steel magnate, planned his mill would produce primarily steel rails to meet the growing demand in the western United States, as

Left: Norwegian Independence Day in Tacoma, 1914. Tacoma Public Library photo   Below: Japanese have a history of truck farming and marketing in the area, photo circa 1922 Tacoma. Tacoma Public Library photo   Below left: Coal miners at Newcastle in its heyday. Museum of History & Industry, Seattle, WA photo

well as in China and South America. Many of the necessary facilities were in place by the early '90s, but the mill produced not a single rail, no doubt a great blessing, as belching blast furnaces and towering stacks somehow seem inconsistent with pleasant, suburban Kirkland. Yet the city managed to become the main nucleus of the eastern Lake Washington area, just as Renton did on the south shore.

Bellevue and other centers along the eastern Lake Washington shore also were present in the 1870s. However, Bellevue did not become the focus of the area until after the 1940 opening of the Mercer Island Floating Bridge. Completion of the Evergreen Point Floating Bridge in 1963 meant even faster growth. Bellevue has continued to burgeon and now is the Sound's third largest city.

The first wave of white settlers pushing up river valleys in search of farmland was dominantly of northern European or British Isles stock. The English were most numerous, but there were sizable representatives from Scotland, Ireland and Wales. Many of these, of course, came via the Midwest and New England.

Beginning in the 1870s there was an influx of Scandinavians. Some communities, such as Poulsbo and Ballard, had extremely heavy concentrations of Norwegians. Preston, near Fall City, was almost entirely populated by those of Swedish descent. It was a common saying in Preston that anyone who wasn't a Swede was a foreigner. The Norwegians especially became dominant in boatbuilding and commercial fishing.

With the opening of the coal mines, many were drawn from southern Europe. Among the ethnic groups who settled in Black Diamond were Italians, Austrian-Slovenians and Poles. Yugoslavians also were concentrated in other quarters of the mining district.

Chinese laborers were brought to the West initially to work the gold mines and to build the railroads. Locally they then turned to hop picking, coal mining, laundry work, fish canning and other tasks white laborers shunned. A sharp downturn in the regional and national economy in 1883 left workers unemployed and ready to take the jobs then being done by the Chinese. In 1885 white men fired into the tents of sleeping Chinese hop pickers at Squak Valley (Issaquah), killing several. Confrontations spread to nearby Coal Creek, then to the hop fields of Puyallup. The infamous Tacoma expulsion of Chinese in 1885 and Seattle's disgraceful anti-Chinese riots of 1886 followed.

During the first part of the twentieth century, large numbers of Japanese moved into the river valleys, especially in the Green River Valley at Auburn. They carried on profitable truck gardening operations until World War II and their forced relocation inland. By the time they returned, much of the former truck farming lands had been confiscated, taken by industry or put to other urban uses. Today Seattle still is home to 11,000 Japanese.

World War II also brought in large numbers of military personnel from throughout the nation. Many found the Puget Sound environment to their liking and returned after the war to stay. Others, including Blacks, began to move in to work in defense plants. They also have generally remained and comprise 10 percent of Seattle's population.

Seattle and the Puget Sound area continue to absorb newcomers. Boeing has brought in many, often well-educated. Between 1975 and 1980 alone, 21,000 Asian immigrants, half from Vietnam, Korea and the Philippines, made metro Seattle their home.

Changes linked to in-migration of people from California and the East coast are evident. Some "natives" have been concerned about the Californication of Washington and have tried to promote a lesser, rather than a greater Seattle. East Coast Yankees constitute a visible Yuppie component.

This seems to be a place where all are relative newcomers. Unlike New England or the Midwest where it takes a generation or more to feel at home, even those who have been here for a few years talk as if they were natives. A small group can trace its ancestry to the pioneers, but they are so outnumbered that they have no special claim to blue-bloodedness. Consequently, there is comfortable living space for those of all backgrounds. This could be the primary reason so many so readily adopt the Puget Sound as their own, and why they can so soon become its boosters and protectors.

CHINATOWN AND THE INTERNATIONAL DISTRICT

Almost from Seattle's beginning, the Chinese played an important role. They were hard-working and provided cheap labor much needed on the frontier. They worked at the tougher tasks that few others wanted, in the timber industry, the fish canneries, the fields, the mines, the construction of roads and especially the building of railroads. During prosperous times the white population tolerated the Chinese, but when jobs were scarce, they were viewed as a threat.

Orientals were discriminated against from the start. They were allowed to reside only in certain areas and were assigned menial tasks. Those in Seattle were expected to live in Chinatown, a section then centered on the area between Second and Fourth, and along Main and Washington, historically behind the city's warehouses and mills. This was a convenient area for the Chinese who worked in Yesler's steam mill, but it was overcrowded and was treated much as a separate city within a city.

The merchant class, called Fongs, were the primary rulers of Chinatown. This was upside-down from Chinese society back home, but merchant shopkeepers were the key source for labor contractors, and their establishments also provided important social services for Chinese newcomers to the city.

Relationships between the Chinese and the white communities often were strained. Chinatown was governed largely by Chi-

Right: Both Chinatown and neighboring Pioneer Square benefit from Kingdome-generated shoppers. John Alwin photo

nese, and activities were allowed there that were not tolerated in other sections of Seattle. One consequence was that the southern part of the downtown area became overcrowded and somewhat of an eyesore. Its unattractiveness helped nudge the center of the central business district progressively northward.

The Chinese quarter was derisively called Canton Alley. Its back streets were filled with structures having small rooms, sometimes with only a bunk, and accommodating single Chinese immigrants. Its halls of gambling, prostitution and opium dens are legendary.

During the 1880s, when conflict between the Chinese and other groups was at its height, western Washington citizens behaved much as those elsewhere. Both Tacoma and Seattle passed a "Cubic Air Ordinance" specifically designed to break up Chinese concentrations. In Seattle it became law that each person in a living unit had to have 8' x 8' x 10' of space—unheard of in Chinatown. Anti-Chinese actions went beyond city ordinances. In November of 1885 most of Tacoma's 700 Chinese were unceremoniously forced into boxcars in mid-winter and shipped to Portland. Tensions peaked in Seattle the next year with racial riots and the imposition of martial law with troops patrolling the streets.

By 1910 Oriental population once again was booming. When old Chinatown became

too crowded, a new and even larger Chinese cluster developed farther east and south. This area initially was populated largely by single men, but increasingly accommodated general Oriental population from other nations, including Japan and the Phillipines. Still called Chinatown by locals, the area now officially is known as the International District and includes the section from Yesler Way south to South Dearborn and from Twelfth Avenue South west to Fifth Avenue South. It has withstood being bisected by I-5, the rise of the Kingdome to the west and industrial expansion on the south. The district remains very much a city unto itself. Chinese merchants' power has continued. The community also provides a semblance of its own judicial and police system, the care of its own sick and needy and has developed a distinctive identity.

Today the International District contains an admixture of newcomers from the Orient. Vietnamese, Laotian, Thai and Cambodian residents have moved in, set up shop and live side by side with the Chinese, Japanese and Filipinos. Today most of Seattle's Orientals may live outside the International District, especially on Beacon Hill and in the Rainier Valley, but Chinatown remains a major shopping center for specialty foods and other items, claims the city's best Chinese and Japanese restaurants and still is a center for Seattle's and the Northwest's Asian community. Colorful annual street festivals, art galleries, five newspapers (Chinese, Japanese, Phillipine, Thai and Asian), the Wing Luke Asian Museum, the new Northwest Asian Theatre and the long-established Nippon Kan Theatre, all help perpetuate that role.

Above: The International District is a major shopping center for specialty foods and other items. John Alwin photo Left: Traditional cultural activities keep the International District the focus for Seattle's and the Northwest's Asian communities. Ronald Boyce photo Far left: Troops were required to quell Seattle's anti-Chinese agitation in the 1880s. Museum of History & Industry, Seattle, WA photo

A Walk on the Waterfront

Where the sea meets the city. Early-morning sun illuminates Seattle's watery front yard. Joel W. Rogers photo

Walking the Seattle waterfront is such a colorful and vibrant experience the author felt it was best described in the first person. (Ed.)

My mid-June harborfront tour began at the U.S. Coast Guard station at Pier 36 on the southern leg of Elliott Bay and took me northward approximately four miles to Terminal 91 at Smith Cove. Here is Seattle's front porch, or front yard, the city's water-oriented face. It tells us much about the city's past and present, its problems and prospects and the personality that makes Seattle such a special place.

It seemed appropriate that I begin at the U.S. Coast Guard station since this is the control center for movement of all ships plying the waters of Puget Sound. As I parked my car on Alaskan Way South, the uniformed workers were scurrying to check in for shift change. From here, over 1,000 Coast Guard workers rally to rule the waters of Puget Sound and beyond. As homeport for two ice-breakers that see duty in polar waters, a buoy tender and two other large cutters, some personnel see duty well beyond the entrance to the Sound. At the docks the small Coast Guard patrol craft were being readied for the day ahead. This Friday, as with all nice-weather, summer weekend beginnings, thousands of pleasure craft of every conceivable size, shape and condition would soon be converging on the Sound.

But it was the commercial vessels that were keeping the attention of the personnel on the fourth floor of the main building. Here a half dozen people attend ten radar screens monitoring the Sound from Port Angeles to Olympia. The Vessel Traffic System (VTS) requires all commercial vessels to maintain contact. Officer Currier ventured there would be more than the usual 700 vessel contacts today. In all, there were to be 32 freighters, 5 tankers, 93 tugs with tows, 10 military vessels and over 440 ferry crossings, plus various other vessels.

The *President Jefferson* had just arrived at American President Lines (APL) with its load of containers. From Tacoma, the Alaska-bound *Newark* was leaving from the new Sea-Land container facility. Likewise, the *Taikai Maru* out of Tacoma with its cargo of logs was underway for Yokohama, Japan. From the Duwamish waterway, the *Samick Pacific* would leave later in the day to carry its container cargo to Canada. Several oil tankers were in Sound waters and were being assisted by tugs. Navy ships would move later in the day from Bremerton to the terminal at Manchester near Port Orchard. And a large Navy tug was on a path from the nuclear submarine station at Bangor to a berth at Bremerton.

Commander Richard Wright pointed out that this was not even the busy season. That occurs between September and December during the commercial salmon-fishing season when several thousand fishing vessels, many from Alaska, operate in Puget Sound.

As I walked northward, I immediately encountered two of the Port of Seattle's large container cargo terminals, Terminal 37, leased by the Japanese Six Lines (Japan Line, "K" Line, Mitsui-O.S.K. Lines, NYK Line, Showa Line and Y-S Line) and adjacent Terminal 46, leased to American President Lines. (APL will complete a move to the larger and modernized Terminal 5 in 1987.) Almost 100 acres is taken up by these two shippers alone.

Container operations, introduced in the 1960s, are major money generators. Although amounting to about two-thirds of the harbor's tonnage, the Port reports container cargo (more than a million containers in 1984) generates 80 percent of the

Since the 1896 arrival of the Japanese ship, Miike Maru, *the Port of Seattle has maintained important trade links with the Orient. Port of Seattle photo*

Port's 25,000 maritime shipping jobs. Unlike bulk cargo, which is highly mechanized and employs few workers, containers require considerable labor. Containers must be off-loaded, on-loaded, yard managed and trucked to rail.

Even so, it should not be assumed that the container operations are hustling and bustling with workers. Instead they have an almost placid appearance. The yards are clean and neat. Truck-size containers are stacked behind wire fences like giant colored blocks. Trucks come and go in a steady stream. Compared with earlier days, there is little noise and seemingly little action.

Containers are self-contained storage units, varying in size, but with the 20-foot and 40-foot units most common. They are weatherproof, fully secure and, in the case of refrigerated containers called reefers, carry their own cooling systems. No wharf buildings are required and there is nothing much to be seen except the containers. Even workers handling them do not know what is inside.

The most imposing feature of container yards is the giant container-cranes that load and unload the ships. The Port owns about two dozen of the behemoths. Between them, Terminals 37 and 46 have five of the 40-ton-plus capacity cranes. Costing more than $3 million each, they are rented by the hour. About one container is handled every three minutes by a crew assigned to each crane. The goal of APL is to on-load or off-load about 800 containers in eight hours. With their ships carrying up to 2,500 container units, off- and on-loading can be time consuming, despite all the mechanization.

Up to 80 percent of all containers arriving at the Port are transshipped through the intermodal yards by rail to what Seattleites call the "east," meaning anywhere east of Spokane. Seattle Harbor is the West Coast's top Asian gateway port for import of containerized consumer goods for the Midwest and East. Innovative inland transport, including Burlington Northern's double-stacked trains, are helping to make sure the odds are good that a Sony television purchased in Chicago or a

At Terminals 37 and 46, tidy, efficient container yards generate millions of dollars of revenue for the Port of Seattle on a site that once lay under water. Port of Seattle

Hitachi stereo bought in New York City passed through the Port of Seattle. Cargo not sent onward is distributed locally and statewide by truck. Containers exported are filled with military cargoes and electronic equipment, but also with hay, lumber, paper and paper products and fish. On this day about 100 reefers carrying cherries grown in eastern Washington would be on-loaded for Japan. The Port of Seattle estimates that each container ship visit boosts area earnings by $656,000.

It was hard to believe that all about me was *created* land. Formerly the area was tideland, hidden under shallow waters of Puget Sound. The nearby railroad switching yards, the container yards and the entire port area to the west are all fill lands. Across the East Waterway is Harbor Island, the largest man-made island in the world at the turn of the century. This mile-long by half-mile-wide island now is the heart of the Port, which also has facilities farther up the Duwamish and north along the waterfront.

It was on this site, after World War I shipbuilding folded, that infamous Hooverville, analogous to Hollywood Flats in Tacoma, took root. Throughout the Great Depression, Hooverville reigned supreme as a massive shantytown complex of the unemployed. It consisted of a vast menagerie of structures, ranging from cardboard hovels to rather elaborate shacks. It ran its own affairs and was almost a city within a city, having its own "mayor."

The pace and cleanliness of the container sites were rudely broken as I approached Pier 48. The southwest corner of the pier houses the Port of Seattle's Information and Observation Center, but most people know this as the Alaska Ferry Terminal, the southern terminus of the Alaskan Marine Highway System. This state-operated passenger and freight service between Seattle and southeast Alaska makes a trip northward once a week in summer and twice weekly in winter. It was 7:00 a.m. and the ship, *Columbia,* had arrived from Skagway, Juneau, Sitka, Ketchikan and other Alaskan ports. Dozens of stretching, weary and wandering people were venturing off the ship. Some carried duffel bags, others drove off in campers. To their south, visitors were greeted by the neatly stacked containers, to their east stood the two-tiered, dark, noisy and massive Alaskan Way Viaduct. Behind it could be seen the large and, from this vantage point, less-than-attractive Kingdome. To their immediate north a dozen or so transients were sleeping it off on the benches of a small park and even on the boat dock.

As I walked north with some of the disembarked from the *Columbia,* I could see ahead the lure of the waterfront tourist mecca. On this end is the more functional Pier 52, the Washington State Ferries Terminal (Colman Dock). This once was the focus of the Mosquito Fleet, but today handles huge ferries sailing to and from Bremerton and Bainbridge Island on the west side of the Sound. Unloading was the morning rush hour of commuters to Seattle.

Above: Mosquito Fleet steamers, Indianapolis, City of Everett, Burton, Reliance, Kitsap *and* Defiance *await their rush-hour passengers at Seattle's historic Colman Dock. The clock tower dates this photo as pre-April 25, 1912. That night the Alaska Steamship Company's* Alameda *rammed the dock, toppling the clock tower, which was found the following day bobbing in Elliott Bay with its hands stopped at 10:23. The tower promptly was replaced with a taller one on the other side of the structure. Today the Colman Dock is Pier 52, home of the Washington State Ferries. Williamson Collection, Puget Sound Marine Historical Society, Inc., Seattle, WA photo*

Far left: An early-day predecessor of today's ferry schedules. On the back cover of this Eagle Harbor Time Card, the Winslow Dock Grocery advertises its First-Class Soda Fountain and items from mince meat to hardware, hay and grain. Museum of History & Industry, Seattle, WA photo Left: Steamer Tacoma, *a fast steel passenger boat of the Mosquito Fleet at the Tacoma waterfront as depicted in the penny postcard era. Courtesy of Ann Alwin Below: Early 20th century ferry passengers disembark from the* Vashon *at the Island. Williamson Collection, Puget Sound Maritime Historical Society, Inc., Seattle, WA photo*

EVERGREEN FLEET

Although not the dominant connector of years past, the waters of Puget Sound still provide important linkages. The Mosquito Fleet is gone, but today's Washington State Ferries serve as the state's marine highway system, annually transporting more than 7 million vehicles and 17 million passengers over its Puget Sound routes.

Regular ferry service developed early in the Sound, with the first "double-ender" beginning in 1888 between downtown Seattle and West Seattle (allowing horse drawn wagons and carriages to enter one end and go out the other). In 1914 the first ferry specifically designed to carry horseless carriages was launched. During the early Mosquito Fleet years, however, most of the hundreds of privately owned steamers were designed only to carry people and cargo, not vehicles. With the increased competition and growing popularity of the auto in the early twentieth century, smaller operators were squeezed out and a major consolidation of routes and companies took place. The Puget Sound Navigation Company, better known as the Black Ball Line, emerged as the dominant concern. By 1929 it operated 25 vessels on 17 routes. With the demise of its number one competitor in the early Thirties, the Black Ball Line ruled the waves in Puget Sound. Determined to take full advantage of his monopoly, Alexander Peabody bought the entire 17 auto-carrying vessels from the ferry company that formerly served the route spanned by the new Golden Gate Bridge in 1937.

By the late Forties the Black Ball Line and its fares became the "ferry issue" in Washington and were even a factor in the defeat of an incumbent governor. In 1950 the state purchased the Black Ball Line, and the next June Washington State Ferries began operating with 16 craft and 20 terminals.

Many of the routes remain the same today, with the exception of two made unnecessary by bridge construction, and the acquisition of the Port Townsend-Keystone run. The system still uses four of the Golden Gate Ferries acquired more than 40 years ago. A most notable change is the size of newer vessels, including the four, 392-foot Super Class and the two, 2,000-passenger, 206-auto capacity Jumbo Class craft.

In the late Eighties the Evergreen Fleet consists of 22 vessels serving eight routes. With the 4,799,621 passengers and 1,633,272 autos it conveyed across the Sound in 1985, the commuter-dominated Seattle-Winslow (Bainbridge Island) link is the system's unchallenged volume leader. Claiming between 2.2 and 2.8 million riders each, the Seattle-Bremerton, Edmonds-Keystone, Fauntleroy (Seattle)-Vashon, Southworth and Mukilteo-Clinton vie for second ranking. The state estimates that each year the ferries save car drivers over 570 million miles of highway driving and the Puget Sound region 26,000 tons of vehicle emissions.

For most regular users, like Professor Howard Mount of Seattle Pacific University, the ferries provide an economical and welcomed shortcut between their homes and places of work. He is one of several of the school's faculty and staff who commute daily via ferry between Bainbridge Island and downtown Seattle. Each morning he leaves his automobile at the Winslow dock and boards the ferry as a walk-on passenger. Upon docking at Pier 52 he picks up his second vehicle, garaged near Ivar's Acres of Clams, for the 10-minute trip to campus.

The typical travel day for Howard begins by dropping his children at their Bainbridge Island school in time for him to catch the 7:45 a.m. Seattle ferry. By 8:40, approximately an hour and 20 minutes after leaving home, and after having spent 35 minutes aboard one of the Jumbo Class ferries, the *Spokane* or the *Walla Walla,* he arrives at work. In the evening, he leaves Seattle Pacific about 4:15 p.m., sprints for the 4:40 ferry and arrives back at Winslow at 5:15 p.m. Says Mount, "The sprint is the stock in trade of all ferry riders. Running down Alaskan Way, sometimes only to miss the 4:40 is part of the routine." On those days he must wait for the 5:25. Ordinarily his arrival time at work and at home is as precise as a German train.

Mount does not consider the ferry ride part of the commute time. To him the ferry is an important space for work and preparation, either for the city or for his return home. "I have my own 'reserved' table, the place I always sit," he says. "It's a quiet time."

"Ferry commuters can be classified into three types," says Mount. "There are the talkers and chatterers, each morning gathering in their accustomed spots to share jokes and current events. These, like all of us, have become experts on how best to run the ferries. Then there are the card players, usually bridge. Finally there are the workers, like me." Regardless of the group, all are dressed in business attire. Tourists are almost non-existent during commute time. But Mount does not really know anything about the people with whose faces he is so familiar. "I occasionally run into people from the ferry when I'm in the city. We say 'Hi,' but I know nothing about them."

By purchasing a Frequent User Book with script for 20 one-way passages, Mount can ride as a pedestrian round-trip for about $2.00 a day. Those who drive their auto aboard pay about $9.00. For years Professor Mount rode a motorcycle to cut costs and have transportation on the Seattle side. "A surprising number drive," he says. "Some need their cars to get to their jobs in the Seattle suburbs; others are simply rich!"

In the ten years that Mount has been riding the ferry he has had some exciting times. As with other cross-Sound ferry commuters, the glory moments come on those clear days when Mount Rainier looms large and clear over Elliott Bay. "Although I get rather accustomed to the view and generally ignore it, on those days the mountain is absolutely awe-inspiring," says Mount. There are times when killer whales and seals splash around the boat. Mount likes to pass near the cruise ships that occasionally enter Seattle waters.

When weather is windy or foggy, difficulties sometimes arise. "Once we almost

collided with a freighter. The captain threw the boat into full-reverse fast. We missed it by only a hundred yards. One night we rescued two gillnetters from their burning boat." On other occasions the commuters have been greeted in Seattle by a mangled dock, damaged by one of the new computer-controlled Super Ferries, and even by cars lying deep in the water, having been driven off the pier.

An almost routine crisis is the periodic birth of babies. There being no hospital on Bainbridge, each expectant mother keeps the ferry schedule handy during her last months of pregnancy. "Several women a year don't make it all the way to Seattle," says Mount. "Physicians seem strangely absent during these moments. Maybe doctors don't ride the ferries," a smiling Mount suggests. Contrary to local lore, a baby born aboard one of the Washington State Ferries is not entitled to free passage for life.

One thing brings fear into the hearts of all ferry commuters: not having ferry service at all. The key word is "strike." Mount still is shaken by the last one. "It was chaotic. They brought out the 'Mosquito Fleet'—the harbor tour boats, *Goodtime I* and *Goodtime II*. But service was irregular, prices were higher and there were lines and waiting. I decided to opt for the 92-mile drive-around to work, southward across The Narrows Bridge to Tacoma then up Interstate 5 to Seattle. I got up early and spent most of the strike time driving. It was a nightmare."

Facing page: Officials estimate that Washington State Ferries, the nation's largest system, annually saves motorists more than 570 million miles of highway driving. John Alwin photo
Below: The combination of riding a Jumbo Class ferry, like the Spokane, *and taking in the beauty of the Sound and its breathtaking mountain backdrops is enough to raise adrenalin levels in any novice, but the experience is one regular commuters take in stride. Joel W. Rogers photo*

I next entered the central waterfront section, a magic land of tourists, denizens from Downtown and a menagerie of people types. And, although the sidewalks were still nearly empty, the joggers already were out and about. For the next mile the waterfront consists almost entirely of fish-and-chip joints, import shops and general recreational diversions for in-towners and out-of-towners.

Along this tourist strip are several harbor tour lines (something well worth doing), Waterfront Park, assorted restaurants and shops and other functions that now occupy the otherwise obsolete old wharfs of the tall-masted ship era. Here at Pier 59 next to Waterfront Park is the Seattle Aquarium with its emphasis on sea life of the Puget Sound region. The view into the aquarium from the Underwater Dome is a highlight for most visitors. Opposite the aquarium is the steep, 155-step Pike Street Hillclimb to popular Pike Place Public Market.

Some of the piers are undergoing extensive remodeling, but the past is not to be forgotten. One of the objectives in the harborfront corridor is to remind visitors of the waterfront's past. Plaques, strategically placed, help convey information and enhance the historic perspective. One company proclaims that its tour vessel is the last of the original Mosquito Fleet. Other plaques and signs note that it was at the Waterfront Park that the Japanese ship *Miike Maru* provided the first scheduled steamer service to Japan in 1896, thereby making Seattle an international port. Historic Pier 58 is commemorated by another plaque in Waterfront Park that tells passersby this is where the *Portland* docked on July 17, 1897 with its "ton of gold," the spark that ignited the Klondike Gold Rush. Across the street, vintage Australian trolley cars provide service along the waterfront and connect the northern part of the tourist strip to Pioneer Square, the restored birthplace of the city.

Tourism is big business in Seattle. According to the Seattle-King County Convention and Visitors' Bureau, tourism generates about $1 billion annually for Seattle. The primary places frequented by these out-of-towners are the waterfront strip, Pioneer Square and Pike Place Market. Only the Space Needle, a 1962 World's Fair landmark at Seattle Center, is a major contender for attention.

Right: The venerable and durable Virginia V, *now a tourist attraction on the Seattle waterfront, is claimed by its owners to be one of the original Mosquito Fleet ferries. John Alwin photo   Below: Cruise ship* Pacific Princess *departs the harbor in full regalia. In 1986 Seattle became homeport for this star of the "Love Boat" TV show. The same year, highly regarded Sitmar Cruises homeported its 925-passenger luxury ship,* Fairsea, *at Seattle's Terminal 30 for its Alaska cruise season. Joel W. Rogers photo*

The massive, new and impressive offices of the Port of Seattle at Pier 66 stand out ahead. At 8:00 a.m. some of the 500 employees were arriving. They account for about half the Port's employees. These are the first round of workers who gain their livelihood from the money generated by Port revenues. It is estimated that Port activities generate 70,000 related jobs in the county and 100,000 jobs statewide.

The Port of Seattle, formed in 1911 as one of the nation's first public ports, levies taxes, purchases land and generally administers most port facilities in the Seattle area. In addition to accommodating maritime shipping facilities, the Port also operates Fisherman's Terminal on Salmon Bay, the premier facility serving the Pacific Northwest fishing fleet, and a 1,500-boat-capacity yacht marina on Shilshole Bay. The Port also owns and runs Sea-Tac, among the nation's top 20 airports in terms of annual passenger-traffic volume, exceeding 10 million for the first time in 1984.

As recently as 1984, the Port of Seattle was the second largest container cargo port in the United States. This must be attributed to active promotion of port business and foresight of port officials who 20 years ago could see the future dominance of containerization. Its main rival on the Sound, and one of long standing, is Tacoma. With the 1985 move of the Sea-Land container terminal business to the Port of Tacoma (their administrative and sales office remained), Seattle lost almost one-third of its container business and dropped in ranking to fifth place among U.S. container ports.

As a kind of counterweight to the Alaska Ferry terminal to the immediate south of tourist row, the British Columbia Steamship Company provides daily passenger service to Victoria, Canada during its May-September season. As I arrived at Pier 69, the *Princess Marguerite* was just leaving for its daily round-trip trek to Victoria. The restored 1948 steamer with Union Jack stacks can accommodate 1,800 passengers and 50 autos. This leisurely passage allows one to leave Seattle in early morning, shop, and have tea at the stately Empress Hotel and return the same evening. For those in a hurry to get to Victoria, there also is the *Island Jetfoil*, which can have you enjoying the English charm of that city in just two hours.

Pre-tourist Seattle waterfront at the foot of Columbia Street, circa 1901. Washington State Historical Society, Tacoma, WA photo

During the tourist season a carnival atmosphere prevails on today's waterfront. Joel W. Rogers photo

Next door the vintage 1902 Ainsworth and Dunn dock (Pier 70) marks the end of the central waterfront's active tourist zone. In the 1970s it was renovated and offers shoppers numerous stores, eateries, galleries and fishing charters.

Except for an adjacent small dock, this marks the end of the finger-like piers for almost another mile northward along the waterfront. The shoreline immediately opens into the grass-laden Myrtle Edward and Elliott Bay parks, built on fill land about 100 yards wide between the railroad tracks and the bay. They provide over a mile-long trail along the waterfront.

The Port's primary purpose in developing this extensive park and fill was to provide space for its massive grain terminal at Pier 86. Opened in 1970 and operated by Cargill, Inc., its elevators and terminal facilities handle grain from areas from the Midwest to eastern Washington and provide stiff competition for Portland, Oregon, the Northwest's dominant grain exporter. Ships up to 1,400 feet long and drawing 70 feet can be accommodated. In 1980, the record year, this terminal loaded nearly three million tons of grain. That is enough to fill the cavernous on-site silos more than 25 times or, stated another way, sufficient grain to fill a 290-mile-long train of almost 30,000 grain hopper cars.

Farther north in Smith Cove at the base of Queen Anne Hill are the large, 139-acre Piers 89 and 90 (Terminal 91). The *Victory Age* was docked and Japanese-made cars were being driven off by car jockeys. Forty or fifty persons were driving vehicles off-ship to the adjacent storage yard. The jockeys then were picked up in vans and shuttled back to the ship for the next round. The cars eventually would be loaded on rail and shipped to the Midwest and beyond. This break-bulk terminal also handles fresh fruit, frozen meats, fuel and oil.

Beginning my southward trek back to my car, several things occurred to me. First, the Oriental trade connection plays a most dominant role in Seattle's economy. In fact, Pacific Asia trade makes up 94 percent of the Port's foreign waterborne trade by value and 75 percent by tonnage. Secondly, the connection to Alaska is strong, and it is easy to understand how the Port has earned the nickname, "Alaska's General Store." Although the major out-shipment of items to Alaska occurs in early spring, evidences of Alaskan connections are found all along the waterfront.

But perhaps most interesting is the prominence of the harborfront's north and south for commercial trade as contrasted with the central portion. The site selected by pioneers Denny, Boren and Bell is now the least viable for port use, its old piers inadequate for today's merchant vessels and space unavailable for requisite container yards. In this central zone adjacent to the central business district, a carnival atmosphere dominates. Today the old waterfront buildings are haunted by tourists trying to find the "real" Seattle, Seattle as it was presumed to be. Yet they show little interest in the present adjacent port. It made me wonder how one can appreciate the present if one simply glories in the past.

In Seattle next century, the tourists may well glory in the heady port days of car jockeys, massive cranes and container-ships. What a pity visitors and natives alike don't see the real thing now.

Epicenter of the Emerald City

The central business district of every American city constitutes its royal jewel. Here is held its heritage and its hopes for the future. One corner of the downtown is usually the birthplace of the city, which becomes almost sacred territory, often dedicated to the wisdom of the early pioneers in selecting such a site. It is also in this district, as at Pioneer Square, that most monuments, memories and artifacts of the early city abound.

But if the metropolis is fortunate, near the historic relics are prominent buildings of the present, skyscrapers that outline the profile of the city and stand as monuments of continued success. These temples of commerce form the skyline, creating a distinctive image of each city in the minds of insiders and outsiders alike—the stuff that backdrops to local nightly newscasts are made of.

Since World War II the majestic downtowns of many metropolises have crumbled in ignominious and ragged ruin. One by one, light manufacturing, retailing, restaurants, insurance companies, furniture stores and general offices have abandoned their former homes downtown for the spic and span, up-to-date, open arms of campus-like industrial parks, planned shopping centers and sylvan sites near outlying lakes and treed rolling hills. The consequence is that older buildings were neglected, abandoned or torn down and replaced by parking lots. The vacancies remain as gaping holes in the half-toothless mouth of the metropolis.

Seattle is a grand exception to this rule of ruin. Like Manhattan Island, the Loop in Chicago and certain thriving regional capitals, Seattle has proven to be fertile ground for the sprouting of skyscrapers. Given its majestic hillside site next to Puget Sound, downtown Seattle can be absolutely awe-inspiring.

A peek at the Emerald City from the Westin Hotel. Joel W. Rogers photo

Millions of tourists' cameras have been aimed south off the Space Needle's observation deck to capture Seattle's skyline. John Alwin photo

Of course, central Seattle has paid its tribute to the suburbs. Its once pre-eminent retail area temporarily faded. It has a tenderloin district, its skid row and its share of run-down streets, but clearly it has met the challenge of the automobile, of sprawl and of the surge to the suburbs. During the past decade especially, Seattle has emerged from the battle somewhat bruised but victorious.

On a high-rise binge, more than a dozen new skyscrapers have created an entirely new skyline since 1970. For decades the tallest building west of the Mississippi, and *the* Seattle landmark, was Smith Tower. It now sits at the south end of the CBD as if shunned, dwarfed by a whole forest of new and taller structures. Commerce and tall buildings have moved north, "uptown" to higher ground. Today 76-story, 1.5-million-square-foot Columbia Seafirst Center is Seattle's tallest.

In this office epicenter of the Emerald City are more than 22 million square feet of office space, amounting to more than one square mile if spread out on a single plane. The area in office space has doubled in a decade. Downtown retailing occupies almost another 7.6 million square feet; by comparison, suburban Bellevue Square has 900,000 square feet of retail space. Sales downtown each year amount to over $1 billion, more than any other retail center in the Pacific Northwest.

Not surprisingly, downtown Seattle is the fiscal bulwark for the city's economic base. Here are employed 170,000 people having a payroll of $3.4 billion annually. Forty percent of all jobs within the city are based in the central business district. Consequently, about one-third of Seattle's taxes are generated in this small area occupying only about 1,000 acres, or two percent of the city's land area.

Above: Towering Columbia Seafirst Center dwarfs the coveted Smith Tower, for decades after its mid-Teens completion the tallest building west of the Mississippi. The 76-story monolith will have to satisfy the city's edifice complex since present zoning restrictions should rule out taller structures. Developer Martin Selig, owner of the Columbia Center and many of the newest downtown buildings, has almost single-handedly remade Seattle's skyline. John Alwin photo   Right: Nostalgic 1942 view of Seattle's downtown from Beacon Hill on the eve of a Second World War-induced era of dramatic growth. Museum of History & Industry, Seattle, WA photo

THE UNIVERSITY OF WASHINGTON CONNECTION

Consistent with its role as center of heritage and hope for the future, a section of today's downtown was also the center for higher education in young Seattle. The site of the flagship Four Seasons Olympic Hotel originally was occupied by the Territorial University of Washington. The impressive cupola-crowned and column-graced Territorial University Building was completed in 1861. Its grounds comprised a 10-acre site atop Denny's Knoll on land donated by three founding families, mostly from Arthur and Mary Denny.

Without territorial financial assistance, the early years were difficult ones for Seattle's new educational institution. Initially it was used for instruction at all levels and even as a community hall. It was not until 1876 that the university granted its first college diploma. The next year some territorial funds became available and the future seemed more assured for this oldest state institute of higher learning on the Pacific Coast.

In 1889 the college became the University of Washington, and two years later the cornerstone of Denny Hall was laid on the site of the spacious new campus seven miles northeast of downtown. Even though the campus opened for business in the mid-1890s, the U of W retained ownership of the downtown acreage, now called the Metropolitan Tract, which has expanded to 11 acres.

Not only does the University own the land in the heart of downtown between Union and Spring, Third Avenue and Fifth Avenue, it also owns the buildings in the tract. Included are Rainier Square, the IBM

The cupola-crowned Territorial University building atop Denny Knoll in 1871 from near Second Avenue and Pine Street. Special Collections Division, University of Washington Libraries, Prosch photo, Neg. No. 2298

Building, Four Seasons Olympic Hotel and the Cobb and Skinner buildings. In fiscal 1985 income and interest from the property generated $8 million, which after expenses left $2.3 million cash for the University.

This once small downtown school that struggled for survival in its infancy has blossomed into one of the nation's premier universities. It is justifiably mentioned in academic company with Stanford, Berkeley, the University of Michigan, Ohio State and other most respected of the nation's centers for higher education.

If a Sounder decides to go to a four-year college close to home, chances are he or she will enroll at the "U." With enrollment at Seattle Pacific, Seattle University, Pacific Lutheran and the University of Puget Sound about 3,000 each, none comes close size-wise to the U of W's 34,000 student body. Closest in terms of enrollment is 10,000-student Bellevue Community College.

The University is one of the country's most productive research centers. Rather than specializing in a few fields, it has earned a reputation for excellence across the

Far left: Serene Japanese Gardens at the U of W's expansive Arboretum.   Left: College collage, U of W campus bulletin board.   Below: Once the focal point of the 1909 Alaska-Yukon-Pacific Exposition, Drumheller Fountain is now a central campus landmark. John Alwin photos

board in the sciences, arts and humanities. Year in and year out it is a national leader for the amount of federal dollars granted for research, important for support of the more than 10,000 students enrolled in graduate programs. Its schools of Medicine, Dentistry, Pharmacy and Law have international reputations. With a student-to-faculty ratio of 15:1, better even than some of the area's private universities, the school also provides quality undergraduate instruction.

Literally hundreds of thousands of alumni, many still in the Seattle-Tacoma area, have affectionate memories of waiting in line at the University Bookstore with a stack of texts for the new term, taking a lunch break next to Drumheller Fountain, strolling "University Ave," booking it into the wee hours at the Suzzallo or Odegaard library, or savoring apple pie *a la mode* at the Last Exit on Brooklyn. Of late, the nationally ranked Huskies football team has helped sports fans maintain their emotional ties with the school. *(Ed.)*

The Downtown Districts

The viability and character of downtown Seattle lie in its diverse districts, each contributing in its own way to the central city's vitality. On the south, historic Pioneer Square occupies an area bounded by Columbia and South King streets between Alaskan Way South and Fourth Avenue South. To its south is the Kingdome sports stadium and railroad stations, and to the east the International District. To the north, in vertical contrast, is the office-financial district centered near Third Avenue and Spring. East of the office-financial core and across the freeway, officially out of downtown, is the hospital complex, sometimes called "pill hill." Over a half-dozen hospitals and other medical facilities dot First Hill. North of the office core is the 12-square-block heart of the retail district. West and beyond the First Avenue and Pike Place periphery of the CBD, and cut off from downtown by the Alaskan Way Viaduct, parking lots and railroad tracks, is the Waterfront District. North of Pike Place Market are historic Belltown and the entire Denny Regrade.

The many strange orientations of central Seattle's street system can keep visitors to the inner city generally disoriented and reaching for the aspirin in the glove compartment. The triangular-shaped blocks and oddball street angles cause any wise outsider to immediately make his first purchase a map of downtown.

Within each of the rectangular grids, street names and order are fairly easy to grasp. For example, in the CBD core, avenues run northwest-southeast. First Avenue begins at the bluff edge on the western side. Avenues increase in number and altitude (as any breathless pedestrian will confirm) in a northeasterly direction. North of Yesler Way the northeast-southwest trending streets are remembered easily by the phrase, *J*esus (Jefferson and James) *C*hrist (Cherry and Columbia) *m*ade (Marion and Madison) *S*eattle (Spring and Seneca) *u*nder (University and Union) *p*rotest (Pike and Pine). Some Seattleites say this slogan may have been masterminded by a jealous Tacoman.

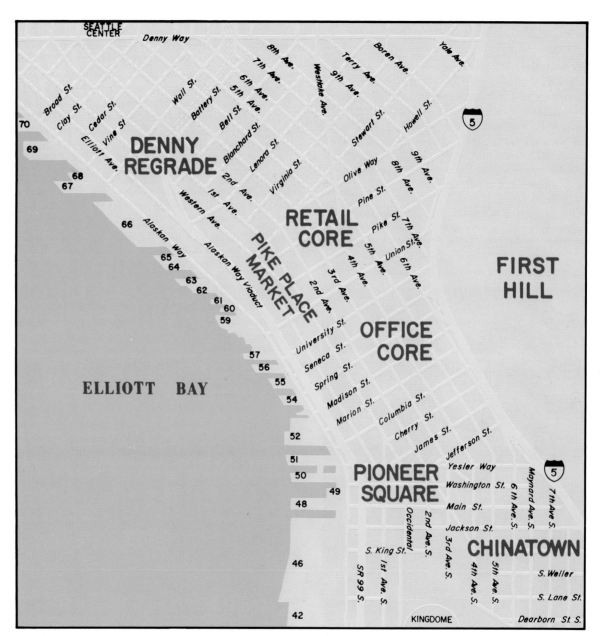

Seattle's downtown and its districts. The legacy of un-coordinated early-day street platting efforts continues today.

PIONEER SQUARE

The first commercial core in Seattle began near First Avenue South and Yesler Way. Following the city's devastating fire of 1889, wooden structures were replaced by more substantial buildings of brick and stone, many of which remain as today's district landmarks. The area boomed in the heady Nineties and early twentieth century in unison with the Klondike Gold Rush. The Klondike legacy in Seattle and Pioneer Square is well presented at the Klondike Gold Rush National Historical Park in the district.

With migration of the city center northward, the district was left in the urban shadow, Seattle's Skid Row. In the late 1960s the area was slated to be cleared to make way for progress, but enlightened citizens rallied to save this heart of old Gold Rush Seattle. It now officially is designated Pioneer Square Historic District. An ongoing restoration effort is succeeding in transforming this into one of Seattle's most exciting communities.

Like much of central Seattle the site of Pioneer Square bears little resemblance to the natural landscape that greeted the first white settlers. In the early 1850s some sections were under water, others were tidal mud flats, and about eight acres of what would become the district's central section made up an offshore island! First Avenue runs along what once was the top of a deeply incised bayside bluff. Gradually low areas were filled and the island buried by the outward extension of land.

The regrade's finishing touches date from the period after the Great Seattle Fire. In an effort to improve sewer service and make sure the area's new-fangled toilets stayed flushed, the city decided that street level (and sewer level) in the quarter would be raised. Over a period of 30 years the task was accomplished, with new street grades raised between 10 and 30 feet. Like an empty moat, a gap the width of the old sidewalks was left between building fronts and the supports for the raised streets. Once new higher-level sidewalks were built, buildings were entered at what previously had been their second or third floors, with lower levels entirely abandoned and earlier sidewalks and storefronts becoming the floors and walls of tunnels—Seattle's underground today. Sections of this approximately 20-square-block buried city are open for 1½-hour tours that begin at Doc Maynard's Public House at 610 First Avenue. Over 100,000 people annually, both tourists and locals, take these excursions, easily the best educational and entertainment buy in town.

Left: Monument commemorating Chief Sealth in Pioneer Square, Seattle's original CBD. Joel W. Rogers photo Above right: An "underground" of a different variety. Touring Seattle's Underground is an eerie, but entertaining, experience. John Alwin photo   Right: The 1890s flavor of Pioneer Square, a designated historic district, is being recaptured through tasteful restoration. John Alwin photo

Above ground, and even in sections of the underground, a revivified Pioneer Square is emerging. As a designated historic district and in accordance with the city's historical preservation laws, all new or remodeled structures conform to the architectural style of the 1890s. Even police, especially during the summer tourist season, may wear Gay Nineties uniforms. Here in an atmosphere of yesterday are an interesting mix of galleries, restaurants, antique shops, taverns, bookstores and other retailers and offices. Renovations also have extended to apartments and condominiums, making way for increasing residential population.

Pioneer Square is not an artificial, sterile tourist trap, fenced off from the rest of the city. Given its recent Skid Row history, an abundance of benches and the continued presence of missions (Union Gospel, Lutheran Compass, Bread of Life and Salvation Army), it should not be surprising that the district is the focus for Seattle's 4,000 homeless. Street people sleeping on park benches and curled up under newspapers beneath trees are part of the cityscape in Pioneer Square.

OFFICE AND FINANCIAL DISTRICT

The rise of skyscrapers reflects Seattle's pride and glory and its growing role as a service center. These are the giant vertical factories of today, filled with white-collar workers instead of the lunch-bucket, hard-hat variety. Here in the central section grows a forest of buildings that makes miniscule the giant Douglas firs that formerly occupied the site.

It is hard to believe that the 50-story Seafirst building, built in the late 1960s, once overpowered the Seattle skyline. The standard and now slightly

Left: Numerous missions serving some of Seattle's 4,000 homeless, such as Big Rex, are part of the scene in Pioneer Square. John Alwin photo   Below: Ailing downtowns of major urban centers have come to be an accepted fact, but Seattle is an exception to the rule. The central city continues to thrive as a retail, office and financial center, its skyline constantly changed by new construction. Joel W. Rogers photo

Right: A downtown Seattle cityscape. John Alwin photo
Below: Downtown reflections. Joel W. Rogers photo

worn joke is that this was the black box in which the Space Needle arrived. The once controversial Seafirst building stood head and shoulders above all other structures, and some planners disliked it immensely. Its domineering presence, they said, did not complement other structures; it was far too tall and should never have been allowed. They much preferred the style of the Smith Tower, which they thought better reflected the image and essence of the city. Today the Seafirst building is eclipsed by other edifices, one among many in a grove of high-risers now crowned by the new Columbia Seafirst Center.

There are so many skyscrapers in the CBD that even the natives cannot keep them straight. Next time you take your out-of-town visitors to Hamilton Viewpoint Park on Duwamish Head for a view of the skyline across Elliott Bay, ask others there if they can name the buildings. Chances are they will be able to identify only the venerable Smith Tower (and probably will even be able to tell you some of its lore), the Columbia Seafirst Center (locals often forget to include its middle name), and the now partially hidden Seafirst building.

The city's new downtown plan calls for this 30-block office core west of I-5, south of Union and east of Second Avenue to remain the primary concentration of high-rise offices. To prevent over-development of the core, some new office buildings under 40 stories will be targeted for adjacent areas immediately to the north and south.

Each new large office complex can mean thousands of additional downtown commuters clogging already crowded arterials and adding to the downtown parking dilemma. The Columbia Seafirst Center alone brought more than 5,000 new employees to the CBD. To help alleviate the transportation problem, construction of a 1.9-mile-long, twin-tube bus tunnel is scheduled to begin in 1987. The transit tunnel, with its half-dozen stations, will underly Pine Street from I-5 to Third Avenue and then proceed south under that avenue to the International District. It will accommodate commuter diesel buses from outlying areas that will switch to electric power upon entering the tunnel. The plan is to reduce street congestion in the downtown area.

Another Bellevue tower reaches skyward in a spic and span CBD amplified by extensive use of reflective glass. Downtown Seattle long had a near-monopoly on central office and financial services, but burgeoning downtown Bellevue now offers some competition. John Alwin photo

BURGEONING BELLEVUE: EAST SIDE COMPETITION

First-time visitors to the Seattle area driving north out of Renton on Interstate 405, might easily mistake the impressive cluster of high-rise buildings just ahead to be downtown Seattle. A quick glance at the road map reveals that this is, instead, suburban Bellevue's shining CBD. Although still considered a Seattle suburb, fast-growing Bellevue is the state's fourth largest community. It is rapidly evolving beyond suburban status and becoming the regional focus for the burgeoning and affluent East Side.

Mushrooming population growth in Bellevue is a recent phenomenon. Until the 1940 opening of the Mercer Island Floating Bridge, Lake Washington isolated this East Side community from its urban parent to the west. From the late nineteenth century until then, small ferries provided the only direct Seattle links to this rolling and sparsely populated farming and lumbering area. A ready market in Seattle for vegetables and berries, especially strawberries, made agriculture rewarding.

In 1940 the area that would become today's Bellevue had a population of about 2,500, almost 30 percent of which was classified as rural-farm. The floating bridge linking the area to Seattle via Mercer Island broke the region's isolation and sparked economic and population growth. Bellevue incorporated in 1953, and by 1960 had grown to 12,809 within the then less expansive city. The pace of growth quickened in the Sixties with the completion of Evergreen Point Floating Bridge. Participating more fully in the suburbanization of Seattle, Bellevue grew from 12,809 to 61,102 by 1970, a whopping 377 percent increase.

The city's sparkling CBD is perhaps the most obvious evidence of a new Bellevue. Here is a suburb that has decided to become an urban place in its own right. Where others have failed, experts think Bellevue may be a role model for suburb-to-city transformation. A proliferation of 20- to 30-story glass and steel high-rise buildings more than doubled downtown office space between 1980 and 1985 when CBD employment reached 20,000. An ongoing building boom insures both the number of downtown jobs and office space will more than double by the end of the century.

Bellevue is very much in tune with America's rapidly changing economy. It and neighboring Redmond are Puget Sound's leaders in advanced technology. Redmond's Sundstrand Data Control, a manufacturer of aerospace and electronic equipment, employs over 1,500 in the city, and Microsoft adds another 1,000. Bellevue is home to Boeing Computer Services with its 1,240 employees, plus other high-tech firms, including Control Data.

In addition to having high-tech research and development and associated light manufacturing, Bellevue also is a major service center. With corporate headquarters located in the city, Pacific Northwest Bell and Puget Sound Power and Light combine for over 2,000 jobs. Given the ongoing and anticipated growth and the East Side's 330,000 residents, many with above-average incomes, it is not surprising that Bellevue is an increasingly important financial center. The new 24-story Rainier Bank Plaza, Pacific First Plaza and others are earning downtown's 108th Avenue the nickname, Financial Row. The anticipated Seafirst Building at planned, futuristic (even by Bellevue standards) Bellevue Place adds impetus to the arrival of the city as a major commercial hub.

Bellevue is not merely an economic entity of new high-tech plants and high-risers. It is home to the Pacific Northwest Arts and Crafts Fair, the largest outdoor fair of its kind in the nation and a Bellevue tradition since 1946. The city also has the Bellevue Art Museum, which mounts international exhibits and boasts an excellent permanent collection of regional works. Reminders of the pre-boom era can be seen in Old Bellevue, where cobblestone sidewalks and flower baskets evoke a traditional Main Street charm. Park-like suburban neighborhoods, including Norwood Village, Wilburton and Robinswood, an abundance of city parks, and beaches along Lake Washington all add to the city's livability.

All indicators suggest more of the same for burgeoning Bellevue. If trends continue, population in the East Side area will exceed 450,000 by the year 2000 and will surpass that of the city of Seattle.

By concentrating commercial development in its CBD, Bellevue has been able to spare its residential areas from rampant commercialism. They remain largely treed and peaceful suburban neighborhoods. Still, the community is not without its growing pains. Traffic at times can be impossible as thousands of workers head to their high-rise office jobs on streets designed for station wagons carrying suburban housewives, 2.2 children and the family dog downtown to shop. Some former Seattleites who earlier had moved to suburbia to get away from traffic and congestion are less than pleased with Bellevue's rapid growth. Many would have preferred it remain strawberry fields forever.

RETAIL CORE

By the early Seventies, retailing in downtown Seattle, like central business districts throughout the nation, had taken a double decade of beating. Almost all furniture establishments had moved to the suburbs, several of the mainline department stores were out of business and those remaining had opened branches in outlying areas. It soon became evident that Seattle might go the way of many other downtowns—a deteriorating complex of has-been stores primarily serving the nearby low-income populations. In 1972 all of downtown Seattle generated only $200 million in sales. Today, thanks to a dramatic retailing recovery, sales are over $1 billion and growing. In the entire city almost one-quarter of all sales is generated in the CBD. With each new major office building even more retail space is added.

Since the inception of retailing in Seattle, there has been a movement to the north. By the early 1900s the center of retailing had moved northward to about the First and Yesler area. By the mid-Thirties the focus rested near the present-day Woolworth store at Third Avenue and Pike. Today it is centered on Pine, between the twin retail anchors, the Bon and Frederick & Nelson.

Just to the east, tree-lined Fifth has emerged as the downtown's most fashionable shopping avenue. Classy Rainier Square in the distinctive Rainier Bank Tower complex is the hub for the avenue.

Above right: Seattle's downtown alleys, terra incognito for most, are frequented almost exclusively by trash pickers and cab drivers taking a short cut. John Alwin photo Far right: The monorail, built for the 1962 World's Fair, provides a speedy and inexpensive link between the downtown's Retail Core and the Seattle Center to the north. John Alwin photo Right: Break time beside Henry Moore sculpture. Joel W. Rogers photos

Facing page, right: The Rainier Bank Building may be one of Seattle's most photographed structures. Far right: An enticing display at Pike Place. John Alwin photos

60

PIKE PLACE MARKET

No discussion of downtown Seattle is complete without mention of Pike Place Market. While many of the city's landmarks are of the polished and vertical variety, this one is low and a bit scruffy. Therein lies much of its charm.

Begun in 1907 as a place for local farmers to sell directly to their customers, it soon became a multi-level bazaar also offering fresh fish, flowers and agricultural produce from farther afield. In the 1960s this slightly Bohemian section was slated for urban renewal. Citizen action and a 1971 citywide vote saved this Seattle tradition.

Since then tens of millions of dollars of both public and private funds have been used in an extremely successful renewal project. The Market, as locals know it, now is more vibrant than ever. It still offers fresh seafood, flowers and produce, but also is the business address for restaurants and cafes, shops and craftspeople. The Market's smell of fish, its noisy and often crowded aisles with overflowing stalls and the sounds of barkers, street musicians and an occasional ferry whistle combine to give visitors a uniquely Seattle experience.

Facing page: Pike Place at night. John Alwin photo Below: The Market, outside looking in. John Alwin photo Right: Denny Hill Regrade by hydraulic mining methods, Fourth Avenue and Virginia, November 1909. F. G. Lewis, Museum of History & Industry, Seattle, WA photo

THE DENNY REGRADE

For decades after its founding, the northern expansion of Seattle was blocked by Denny Hill, a glacial-age vestige about the size of Queen Anne Hill. Generally too steep for horse-drawn carriages, it lay largely undeveloped until regrading began in the late '90s. Reginald Thomson, city engineer of the time, was the grand master of regrades. He thought Seattle was situated in a pit and saw to it that the city dig its way out.

The Denny Hill undertaking was the most notable among the city's many regrade projects. Beginning on the west side with First Avenue, the hill was leveled in stages. The largest section was removed between 1908 and 1911 using a hydraulic mining technique with water drawn out of Lake Union. The slurry mix of sand and gravel was directed into Elliott Bay via a ditch-tunnel system. Island-like mounds, the last of the hill, were leveled in 1929-30.

Despite its proximity to the heart of downtown, little was done with the 60-block Regrade between Pike Place and Denny Way until the 1950s. The district, easily viewed from the monorail, now is one of Seattle's most diversified. Its interesting mix of high-rise office buildings, apartments and new condominium towers, shops, restaurants and open spaces, and even some reminders from the past, is unique to the downtown.

City planners look to this area, and especially its historic Belltown section, as the last chance to establish a major new residential community downtown. The rapid rate of redevelopment and sprouting of high-rise office complexes has taken its toll of downtown residential areas, especially for low-income people. Today the downtown is home to only about 10,000, fewer than at the turn of the century. The city's new plan encourages development of housing for all income levels within the Regrade, an area planners think has a population potential of 20,000.

SEATTLE NEIGHBORHOODS

As the city's employment, retail, business and entertainment focus, downtown Seattle is a shared neighborhood. Beyond the limits of the CBD is a mosaic of distinctive residential neighborhoods. From Haller Lake and Lake City on the north to Arbor Heights and Rainier Bench on the south, Seattle is more a confederation of neighborhoods than a single city. Although all residents are Seattleites (they would say Seattle is their hometown, if asked), there is a good chance their most intense loyalty is to West Seattle, Queen Anne, Wedgewood or one of the city's other more than 40 discrete neighborhoods.

Each has its own unique identity and personality. Some were incorporated towns before annexation by an outward expanding Seattle and have their own history. Virtually all have a strong sense of community, some small-town qualities and active community action groups ready and able to stand up for their home turf.

People from small towns often wonder how people can live in a large city like Seattle, with its supposed overpowering scale and impersonality. An afternoon in one of Seattle's residential neighborhoods usually is sufficient to show that many aspects of urban life are not that much different than small town living.

Aris Manes has been a waitress at Vann's restaurant in West Seattle for years. She is a native West-Sider and wouldn't think of moving elsewhere. Located at 4542 California in the West Side's "own" downtown, what locals call The Junction, the restaurant has been "serving fine food in West Seattle since 1926," according to the tab each customer receives. Such loyalty and continuity are important qualities in West Seattle.

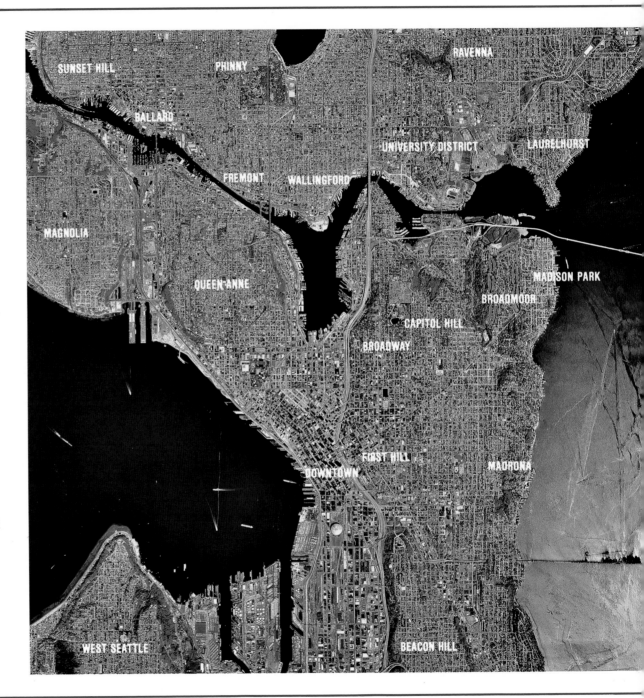

Facing page: Seattle neighborhoods as they appear from an altitude of 40,000 feet. False color, infra-red image such that vegetation shows up as red. The total number of neighborhoods and their boundaries are indefinite. For example, the Neighborhood Statistic Program, compiled by the U.S. Census Bureau, divides Seattle into 97 neighborhoods. U.S. Geological Survey EROS Data Center photo   Right: Each summer for almost 40 years, Florence Cranford and her husband, Donald, have tended what must be West Seattle's most flower-filled yard. John Alwin photo   Far right: The view from the Victorian front porch of the Frederick Betts home on Queen Anne Hill. John Alwin photo   Below: Canal Market has been a neighborhood store in its corner of Capitol Hill since the Twenties. Joel W. Rogers photo

"People are born here, go to school here, have their kids here and die here," says Aris. Her mother still lives in the neighborhood as do her married children. Longterm residence fosters a closeness. She still knows many of her schoolmates from West Seattle High and works at Vann's with the daughter of a friend from her graduating class.

In Vann's people greet each other much as they might in a downtown cafe in Ellensburg or Shelton. Some have been regulars since the Forties.

Despite the recent completion of the West Seattle Freeway, with Seattle's downtown now only 10 minutes away, the close sense of community and neighborliness shouldn't fade. "I haven't been to town [downtown Seattle] for over two years," Aris reports. "We've got everything we need right here." (Ed.)

Tacoma
Second City on the Sound

Tacoma has a mix of activities uniquely Pacific Northwest. Its harbor area affords graphic evidence of the region's traditional resources—timber, fish and grain, and alumina in the giant portside storage domes destined for smelting point to the region's hydroelectric power. Weyerhaeuser, the kingpin company of the timber industry, is most associated with Tacoma and for decades had its headquarters downtown. The Tacoma Dome, constructed of wood, reflects one of the region's great natural resources. Tacoma is equally representative of the Sound because of the important role of the military in the city's history and economy. A less-than-level topography, spectacular mountain backdrop, watery front yard and its friendly, non-urbane citizens make Tacoma exemplary of the Sound.

For most cities all this would be enough to earn accolades from outsiders. Not so in the case of Tacoma, which perennially is compared to Seattle and comes out second. There is something very unflattering about being second in anything. Second rate, second fiddle, secondhand come to mind. Being second suggests being flawed, not quite acceptable. When applied to cities the term denotes some contest waged in which there was a clear winner and loser. The loser, like Cain, carries a distinctive mark of disgrace.

Such has been the long-standing image of Tacoma, a city that can't and couldn't, that once had the audacity to try to be number one. Having had their brief opportunity for greatness, Tacomans muffed it; made their best effort, but didn't have the right stuff. Tacoma carries the indelible image, at least from the perspective of Seattleites, of a never-was or at best a has-been.

A section of Tacoma's downtown from the City Waterway. John Alwin photo

GIG HARBOR

VASHON ISLAND

PUGET SOUND

POINT DEFIANCE

COMMENCEMENT BAY

THE NARROWS

TACOMA

CARR INLET

I-5

PUYALLUP RIVER

McNEIL ISLAND FED. PEN.

STEILACOOM

I-5

McCHORD AFB

FORT LEWIS

Tacoma area from 65,000 feet (about twice the cruising altitude of a commercial jet) just prior to construction of the Tacoma Dome. A false-color image, lush vegetation registers an intense red. U.S. Geological Survey, EROS Data Center photo

The eye-catching Tacoma Dome greets passers-by on I-5.
Jonathan Nesvig photo

No city on the Sound, indeed anywhere in the state if not the entire Northwest, has been more verbally abused. Tacoma gets no respect. Referred to by some residents as a kind of Sodom on the Sound, a sin city, little old dirty Tacoma and Seattle's dirty back yard, this creator of the "aroma of Tacoma" has been kicked around as a matter of habit. It is almost expected that any self-respecting non-Tacoman will have something nasty to say about Tacoma. Taking swipes at the city in some circles has become a hallmark of good taste, sound judgment and a respect for honesty. More than one Seattle politician has parlayed himself into the State Capitol by exposing anew the corruption, vice and seedy centers of sin in Tacoma.

Unfortunately Tacomans have been only too cooperative. Many of their wounds are self-inflicted. Almost every fast-draw of potential success has been followed by a shot to the foot. Until recently being an optimist in Tacoma was almost sufficient grounds for being arrested or at least deported.

It is ironic that the other early contenders for first place on the Sound are far below second place in population, yet Port Madison, Port Blakely, Port Gamble, Mukilteo, Steilacoom and others receive no censure. Tacoma has increased in population in every census and now is the hub for its own metropolitan area of over 500,000. In almost any other context it would be touted as a city victorious.

Given the bigger is better, Barnum and Bailey standard adopted by many today, Tacoma always comes out second to Seattle, a kind of Newark next to New York City, or an Oakland across the bay from San Francisco. Because it lies in the shadow of Seattle and had the gall to challenge it, Tacoma always gets low billing there. Sometimes it gets no billing at all as in 1984 when the Port of Seattle temporarily erased Tacoma's name from Seattle-Tacoma International Airport by changing it to Henry M. Jackson International Airport.

Tacoma does have a checkered, roller-coaster history. A few high expectations were followed by resounding, bottom-of-the-barrel pratfalls. Early settlers by-passed Tacoma because of its lawlessness, a reputation that stuck for decades. During World War II the commander of nearby Fort Lewis threatened to put the entire downtown off limits because of the plethora of illicit activities along Pacific Avenue. To some outsiders it almost appeared that the offshore McNeil Island Federal Penitentiary was situated there so as to be a convenient retirement center for Tacoma politicians. Tacomans are quick to point out that the federal judges in Tacoma had sentenced a fair number of Seattleites to McNeil. Until the new city manager form of government began in the 1950s, corruption in high places seemed the mark of Tacoma.

Even when Tacomans have tried to do right, it often has turned out wrong. Downtown Tacoma is the classic case in point. All efforts to curb the exodus of shopping might best be described as fiascoes: the escalade fiasco, the Broadway Plaza fiasco and the municipal garage fiasco. The result was that in the 1970s urban specialists usually listed downtown Tacoma as a basket case on all fronts—retailing, office and commercial use.

The Tacoma Mall, about 3½ miles south of downtown, also was self-inflicted injury. It was approved by the city even though warned it likely would severely impact downtown. When opened in 1965 the mall quickly outstripped, indeed, denuded, much of the central city. Today the Tacoma Mall boasts five major shopper-drawing department stores, more than any shopping center in the Pacific Northwest. Downtown Tacoma has none.

During the 1970s there was such heated controversy among council members, of which the mayor was key contender, that the stormy meetings were

The Grace Island, *bound for the Orient, takes on logs at the Port. John Alwin photo*

broadcast live. They provided popular radio entertainment for all within ear shot. There were plenty of problems to provide finger-pointing blame for everyone. As usual, Tacoma became a source of amusement and lofty disdain among outsiders.

Because of all this, I didn't have a clue as to what to expect when I went for my scheduled interview with Tacoma Mayor Doug Sutherland. Mayor Doug, as some call him, came bouncing out of his office, coffee cup in hand and a smile on his face. He swept me through his office and out onto the garden patio, stood on a bench and began a monologue on the virtues of the "new Tacoma."

He spoke of those, the best of the oldtimers and the newcomers, who are changing Tacoma to an upbeat place, a dynamic city, viable, having a new spirit and a desire to do. (He did murmur something about some who had not yet been reborn and that perhaps another 50 spiritual funerals would be helpful.) Even so, to him the new aroma of Tacoma had the sweet smell of success. He then began listing a recent record of savory victories.

His hand swung northward to Commencement Bay, considered one of the five best natural harbors in the world and, of course, superior to any others on Puget Sound. He pointed out the shorelands near downtown, the rapidly changing, park-laden and restaurant-dotted Ruston Way, and spoke of plans to extend restaurant and park facilities still farther southward along the waterfront.

He took special pride in the port itself. He mentioned Sea-Land, the largest container shipper in the world, which had moved terminal operations from Seattle in mid-1985. "Seattle told Sea-Land what it expected from Sea-Land; we said, 'What do you need?' Those in Seattle have always had it their own way, but things are different now." He noted the new intermodal (ship-rail) facilities. "Suddenly Seattle is also taking an interest in getting their facility close to the docks, like ours," said the mayor. "They wouldn't have considered it without some competition." He told in moving

69

Above: On the deck at Shenanigan's Waterfront Restaurant. Despite the fact that Seattleites view Tacomans as second-class Sounders, a kind of Puget soundis secondarius, *some from the Emerald City have been known to sneak down to Tacoma's classy new Ruston Way dining establishments.   Above right: Inside the Dome.   Right: Sea-Land's* Endurance, *the first company ship to dock in Tacoma, on its arrival in spring 1985. Jonathan Nesvig photos*

terms how the port had grown from a 240-acre tract of tidelands to a 2,400-acre complex. Each year more than 1,000 ships call at the port, and it is served by over 20 shipping lines.

The mayor's enthusiasm increased as he pointed to the Tacoma Dome, Tacoma's answer to Seattle's non-cooperation with respect to an originally planned joint sports facility between the two cities. It was a great disappointment to Tacoma when Seattle built its own near downtown. Opened in the early Eighties, this largest wooden domed structure in the world is a symbol of Tacoma's rebirth. To date, it has accommodated over three million patrons and, according to Mayor Sutherland, has greatly increased the cultural awareness of Tacomans. The historic and thriving Pantages Centre in downtown Tacoma thrilled him even more. An art connoisseur, Mayor Sutherland is excited about the new Tacoma, a blending of the best of the old and the promise of the new.

The mayor's promoter stance would have surprised him as much as anyone a decade or so earlier. Sutherland was an outsider, an eastern Washingtonian, no less. He grew up in Spokane, went to school at Central Washington College in Ellensburg and in 1965 joined Boeing. His wife began looking for a house and, much to his horror, she selected one in Tacoma. He says his reaction was, "Oh, my God! Not Tacoma!" For the next several years, Doug became one of the thousands who commute daily between Tacoma and the Boeing plants in King and Snohomish counties. As providence would have it, he found himself titular head of what he had earlier viewed as a place to be avoided.

After his enthusiastic account, I thought it time to bring up the touchy question interviewers always ask: What is your attitude about Seattle? "We've got to get people off the kick of making comparisons to Seattle," was his response. "We're not interested any longer in comparing ourselves with Seattle, or any other city on the Sound—each city has its own character. But most importantly, such comparisons diminish our vision of what we aspire to become. We are not interested in being equal in population with Seattle—we do not accept their bigger is better, pile it higher and higher philoso-

Mt. Rainier, originally Mt. Tacoma, looms large over Tacoma's busy Commencement Bay. Jonathan Nesvig photo

phy—we are interested in quality, not quantity. In fact, our comparisons and interests are greater than the Sound; they are global—geographically and culturally. We do not strive to become the biggest population center on the Sound; we think of ourselves as a community connected with the world, especially with the Pacific Rim countries. We don't tell customers what we want; we ask them what they need."

He continued with a smile, "We're happy to cooperate with Seattle when it is mutually beneficial. Of course, those in Seattle now are talking about cooperation. As long as things were going their way, they didn't say much about it. Now that they've lost TOTE and Sea-Land to us and are experiencing some real competition, they suddenly talk about intra-Sound port cooperation. I believe in competition. I think it keeps the pencils sharp. It works against complacency. Sure, we'll cooperate with Seattle."

There is no question about the spacious Port of Tacoma being on the move. In the 1980s it is one of the fastest growing ports in the nation. It bustles with large-scale activity and has more of a distinctive Pacific Northwest flavor than any other Sound port. Mount Rainier dominates the southeastern skyline and sheltered and commodious Commencement Bay lies ready to accommodate the ships of the world.

The port is almost overpowering in scale. It includes the entire lower Puyallup River Delta, stretching over two miles wide and deep between

John Alwin photo

Double-stack trains greatly increase efficiency of rail transport inland from the Port of Tacoma. Port of Tacoma photo by Rod Koon

Bound for the Middle East, Washington State apples await loading at the Port. Port of Tacoma photo by Rod Koon

Facing page: Aging wooden warehouses and factories along the waterfront suggest an earlier era. John Alwin photo

the bluffs at Brown's Point and those at downtown Tacoma. From the air the channelized river and seven man-made waterways look like giant teeth on a garden rake. In addition to the Puyallup River, the northerly Hylebos and Blair waterways reach inland over two miles. Despite extensive new development, the port area still has hundreds of acres available for new uses. Farther up the valley of the Puyallup, still close to the port, are large areas suitable for industrial use—an attribute few major American ports can claim.

Port activities are highly diversified. Massive amounts of manufacturing, impressive breakbulk facilities, container operations, bulk cargo systems for grain, logs and alumina, and some of the most up-to-date loading and unloading facilities in the world are found there.

Tacoma is the nation's number two port for imported rubber (it comes from Indonesia). It also is the foremost container port for Alaska, giving it bragging rights as "Gateway to Alaska," a title formerly claimed by Seattle. Now 65 percent of all cargo bound for Alaska is shipped through Tacoma. The port also is the major handler of imported automobiles in Washington, and the two harborfront grain terminals make it the state's largest exporter, handling grain ranging from eastern Washington wheat to Iowa corn.

On the eastern waterways especially, the port has a hefty Midwestern industrial look. It is reminiscent of Carl Sandburg's description of Chicago,

"stormy, husky, brawly city of Big Shoulders . . . a tall, bold slugger set vivid against the little soft cities . . . bareheaded, shoveling, wrecking, planning, building, breaking, rebuilding . . ."

In contrast some sections of the harbor are sleek, sophisticated, high-tech. The modern Port Administration Building, the nearby World Trade Center and the new container facilities are the antithesis of Sandburg's industrial Chicago image. The port is especially proud of its two state-of-the-art dockside intermodal yards, which eliminate trucking of containers between ship and rail. No other West Coast port has more than one of these prized facilities. In the mid-'80s they added speed and capacity that allowed the port to jump from nineteenth to sixth among U.S. container ports.

Like its rival to the north, the Port of Tacoma constantly seeks improved inland transport links with the nation's marketplace. For example, Burlington Northern now provides port users 65-hour service to Chicago with its double-stack trains. Such speed and efficiency both dockside and for inland transportation were major factors in Panasonic's decision to greatly expand its container freight station operation. Now over 90 percent of all Japanese-made Panasonic consumer goods sold in the United States come through the Port of Tacoma.

As well as being a handler of cargoes, the port and tidelands area also is the major manufacturing district in this traditionally most blue-collar of large Northwest cities. The highly visible Simpson Tacoma Kraft Mill, formerly the St. Regis Mill, is a major employer. Using wood chips from its own timber, other area sources and Canada, the 600-employee plant produces pulp, paper and liner board.

Off the Sitcum Waterway the two giant and sparkling Kaiser Aluminum and Chemical Company alumina storage domes, the "original" Tacoma domes, hold 150,000 tons of Australian produced alumina (a partially processed aluminum

Below: The sometimes aromatic Simpson Tacoma Kraft Mill, a waterfront landmark. John Alwin photo

The Port of Tacoma is a major exporter of Washington logs, most destined for Asian mills.   Above: Here log booms on the Port's Blair Waterway await loading.   Above right: Walking on logs is a skill made safer with spiked foot gear strapped to boots.   Right: Tug boats provide the muscle power to move log booms into position for loading by on-board cranes. John Alwin photos

ore). From here some goes to the nearby 300-employee Kaiser Aluminum Smelter and by rail to the company's reduction works outside Spokane. The Tacoma facility was built by the federal government during World War II to produce aluminum for our war effort, especially important to airplane production at Puget Sound plants. Newly finished Grand Coulee Dam on the Columbia River in eastern Washington provided much of the energy for the power-hungry plant. The Tacoma smelter was acquired by Kaiser in 1947.

Along Tacoma's eight waterways literally hundreds of producers of chemicals, concrete, ferti-

Nalley's products have been associated with Tacoma for generations. Photo circa 1923. Courtesy of Nalley's Fine Foods

lizers, lumber, ships, food, furniture and many other products add significantly to the 23,000-plus manufacturing jobs in Pierce County. A major secondary concentration of manufacturing is inland, strung along South Tacoma Way. Travellers on I-5 cross this industrial area on the Nalley Valley Viaduct. Nalley's Fine Foods, which lends its name to the valley, moved into the area in 1940, after already having been in the city since the Teens. Although now owned by a New York company, Nalley's remains a Tacoma institution. Its 600-employee plant produces a wide range of food products marketed internationally. Included are canned goods, dressings and pickle products, all produced with Pacific Northwest harvests. In Washington the pickles on your Big Mac and the dressing on your fish sandwich at Wendy's are from Nalley's of Tacoma.

Until the mid-1980s another Tacoma-synonymous industry operated on the north side of town, spilling over into the tiny enclave community of Ruston. The 565-feet-tall landmark smokestack still identifies the site of Asarco's former copper smelter and refinery. Working for Asarco has been a family tradition for many in the Tacoma area for over 90 years. Using mostly foreign ores handled by its own waterfront dock, the plant accounted for about 10 percent of the nation's annual copper production before closing. While operational the facility caused significant air pollution, adding a good bit to air quality problems in the city.

Tacoma has paid an environmental toll for its manufacturing tradition. Asarco was the state's top sulfur dioxide producer and annually also spewed 60 tons of poisoning arsenic into the atmosphere. Sulfur dioxide, a by-product of pulp and

Asarco's abandoned smokestack, a North Tacoma monument to a by-gone era. John Alwin photo

paper production, has been emanating from the large harborfront mill for years. New owners of the Simpson Tacoma mill are committed to meeting clean air standards and running as pollution free as possible, but some rotten-egg-smelling hydrogen sulfide releases are unavoidable. Closure of Asarco's smelter, and pollution control efforts at the Simpson Tacoma mill alone have improved air quality. Depending on weather conditions there still can be pungent days in town, but gone are the days when the air downtown was so foul it could be tasted.

The city's Commencement Bay industrial waterways have been labeled by the Environmental Protection Agency as one of the nation's 10 most dangerously polluted sites. A century of heavy industry has piled up bottom sediments spiked with toxic substances, and dredging of the waterways

has transplanted some of the hazardous materials out into the middle of the Bay. Momentum is growing to clean up these pollution hot spots in Commencement Bay and the other almost dozen sites in Puget Sound. Sounders do not want to see their sound become a western version of Chesapeake Bay. A recent survey showed that 72 percent rank Puget Sound pollution the state's top environmental issue.

As if air and offshore water pollution weren't enough, Tacomans recently have been hearing there is a serious pollution threat to their underground water source. It appears that the glacial material underlying the city has allowed industrial pollution in South Tacoma to percolate down into the underlying Clover/Chambers Creek Aquifer, from which pumps draw 45 percent of Tacoma's drinking water.

Despite its substantive industrial sector, the Tacoma area economy is much more dependent on the military. Fort Lewis, McChord Air Force Base, Madigan Army Medical Center and Camp Murray combine to provide over 40,000 jobs, both military and civilian. Sprawling Fort Lewis is the largest installation, accounting for over three-fourths of the employment. In addition there are more than 30,000 military retirees in the area. These payrolls combined amount to over $1 billion annually. Just as Boeing dominates employment in the Seattle area, the military is the linchpin for the general economic health of the Tacoma area.

Even with a diverse and robust economic base and a growing population, it is a city's downtown that sets its image. Here is found the embryo of city origin and the genesis of growth and greatness. It is the skyline of the central business district that provides the city's most distinctive feature.

Efforts are underway to revitalize and spruce up Tacoma's downtown. Paradoxically, much of the most visible change to date has been financed by

Careful attention to preserving the best of the old helps perpetuate Tacoma's unique personality. John Alwin photo

the real estate division of Weyerhaeuser, the homegrown timber giant that moved out of downtown in the 1970s for a new futuristic corporate complex in suburban Federal Way. Weyerhaeuser and other developers took the passage of a 1980 bond issue to build the Tacoma Dome as a sign that the city was serious about change.

Weyerhaeuser's Cornerstone Development Company invested over $90 million in new construction in the first half of the Eighties. By 1985 the south end of Broadway Plaza had the new 16-story Tacoma Financial Center, and across the street the abandoned Sears building and two smaller neighboring structures had been tastefully redone as the Cornerstone Building. Nearby the new 25-story

Tasteful blending of the new with the old is a hallmark of the new downtown Tacoma. Jonathan Nesvig photo

Sheraton Tacoma with its 300-plus view rooms looms large. Not far away, Cornerstone's Tacoma Center Market and Hillclimb add to this Weyerhaeuser-refurbished section of downtown.

Others have sensed the economic promise of the new downtown Tacoma and joined in with additional projects. The old Northern Pacific building has been converted into up-scale office space. Likewise the interesting Old City Hall has been redone into restaurants and offices. A Boston-based company has spent millions redoing the 12-story Rust Building.

The downtown's future as a financial, office and convention center seems much more secure than in years, but the jury is still out on its potential role

Looking east down 11th Street from Fawcett to the 11th Street Bridge and the city's Port and industrial area beyond. John Alwin photo

as a retailing area. It is expected that additional office development will have positive spin-off for retailing as can be seen with some speciality shops. With the Northwest's largest shopping center so close and with talk of another mall in what is now a raspberry field outside Puyallup, the future promises to be challenging for developing the downtown as a retail center. Tacoma may yet be the test case as to whether a central business district can thrive without a sizable shopping district.

What to do with dilapidated and porno-plagued Pacific Avenue remains a major stumbling block to Tacoma's Downtown Renaissance. Until the expected 1988 completion of Interstate-705 into the downtown, Pacific remains the eastern entrance to the central city. The sleazy strip exudes anything but the image sought by New Tacoma promoters. Freeway access to downtown should add to its appeal as a business/financial center, but it may also leave Pacific Avenue in a kind of no-man's land in which redevelopment will be even more difficult.

Tacoma's most loyal supporters admit their town has some scruffy parts, but they see them as evidence of character. Tacoma's cityscape is rich with structures from earlier times. Wise planners and developers sense that it would be foolhardy to destroy all of this historic landscape in pursuit of some antiseptic city of the future. A tasteful blend of past with present seems best suited to preserving the city's identity while still accommodating growth and change.

Public funds already have been used to help save the historic Pantages Theatre, a 1917 vaudeville house that brought Tacoma the Marx Brothers, George Burns and Gracie Allen and W. C. Fields. This meticulously restored facility, now the Pantages Centre for Performing Arts, serves as the focal point for local performing companies and touring shows. Pacific Avenue's abandoned 1911 Union Station, another of central Tacoma's historic gems and the focus of its own historic district, seems destined for restoration and adaptive reuse.

Far left: The classical lines of the Pantages Centre. Left: Tacomans are loyal supporters of their world-class zoo. Below: Although never operated as such, Stadium High School originally was built by the Northern Pacific as a fashionable tourist hotel. Jonathan Nesvig photos

Tacomans are rightfully proud of their city and have no interest in it growing into a Seattle-size community. They prize the many smaller-town qualities and value the fact that, while Tacoma is undoubtedly an urban place, people still have time for each other. The human scale is one with which they are comfortable. The town is still small enough for a simple north, south and east to designate its major districts.

Residents point with pride to a growing list of community accomplishments that would be impressive for a city several times its 160,000 population. The highly visible Tacoma Dome, with seating for up to 30,000, heads the list. Point Defiance Zoo and Aquarium is another feather in the community cap. In 1977 residents voted overwhelmingly in favor of a multi-million dollar bond issue to redo the zoo. By specializing in animals from the Pacific Rim region and using imaginative, nature-like exhibits, the zoo has earned a reputation as a world-class facility. Associated 700-acre Point Defiance Park has its Japanese and formal native gardens, beaches, historic sites, picnic areas and miles of shady drives through hundreds of acres of virgin forests. It is unlike any other municipal park in the country and size-wise is second only to Central Park in New York City.

79

Tacoma is blessed with two first-rate liberal arts colleges—the University of Puget Sound and Pacific Lutheran University. U.P.S. has a highly regarded law school with a branch in downtown Tacoma, and P.L.U. is noted for its excellent schools of Business and Nursing. Both attract an unusually high number of students from outside the area. For the younger set Tacoma also is home to three of the Northwest's dozen or so most respected private schools, 100-year-old Annie Wright School, Bellarmine Preparatory School and suburban Charles Wright Academy.

In Rand McNally's recent *Places Rated Almanac,* Tacoma ranked 112th among the nation's 329 metro areas in terms of livability. It received especially high marks for recreational opportunities (#7), climate and terrain (#12) and the arts (#74). When outsiders who don't know they aren't supposed to like Tacoma objectively evaluate the city, it comes out just fine.

Fishing
A Traditional Puget Pursuit

There are many kinds of fish in Puget Sound of commercial significance, each with its own special catching techniques and history, but it is salmon that provide the mainstay for fishermen. Other types, such as halibut, cod and sole usually are caught in off-salmon seasons and are not as profitable and certainly not as prestigious as the almost sacred salmon. In addition, there are several other aquatic activities, the crab and oyster industries for two, that vie for attention with other fishing endeavors.

With many people equipped with efficient gear all seeking a resource in common waters, the fishing industry understandably has become fully regulated. From its inception, commercial fishing has been intertwined with continuing problems over Indian tribal rights versus non-Indian livelihoods. Today it is regulated as to kind of gear used, seasons and times for fishing and to specific fishing waters. It is also inter-state and international in scale, as between Washington and Alaska, and between U.S., Canadian, Japanese and Russian fishermen in ocean waters.

Those who pursue salmon are the prime fishermen of the Sound. As one gillnetter said when asked whether he caught bottomfish during the off-season, "If I can't make it catching salmon, I can't make it in some other inferior fish." At the bottom of the pecking order is the hake, usually caught by the Russians and by off-season American crab boats pulling trawl nets. Next come cod and sole, then halibut, considered the best of the bottomfish.

Left: Fishing boats, Shilshole Bay, Seattle. Facing page: Mark Schacht aboard the purse seiner, Hydra, *the oldest fishing vessel still operating out of Gig Harbor. John Alwin photos*

There is also a pecking order among fishermen based on the method of catch. Each has special gear, particular boat types and sizes and its advocates. However, the purse seiners usually are considered the most elegant and the trollers (not to be confused with trawlers) the least desirable.

The purse seiner is the largest and most expensive of the salmon-catching craft. Alaskan regulations limit the boat length to 58 feet, and many are precisely that long. They cost several hundred thousand dollars each.

Seining is based on a simple principle. A large net is paid-out of a seiner and put in a circular pattern pulled by a skiff, usually a heavy aluminum vessel powered by a high-horsepower diesel engine. The nets are over 1,000 feet long and about 100 feet wide. When a school of salmon is encircled, the weighted bottom portion of the net is tightened so as to make a "purse." The pursed net then is hauled to the boat by the now ubiquitous MARCO Powerblock.

John and Winona Borovina dockside at Everett. The fishing tradition has always been a part of their family. Ronald Boyce photo

FISHERMAN
JOHN BOROVINA

On a breezy but warm Monday afternoon in late June of 1985, Skipper John Borovina, son of a Yugoslavian immigrant, broke berth at Everett for his annual trek to the fishing grounds of Alaska. Since 1939 John has not missed a single season. From June 30 to August 31 he and his crew of six would remain in Alaskan waters, then, with luck, deposit 25 or so cargoes of fresh salmon at the tender ship serving canneries at Ketchikan, Petersburg and Juneau.

Mr. Borovina's purse seiner, *Star of the Sea,* was accompanied by the *Christian* with sons Tam and Tony, the pilot, aboard. The two boats would join the *Susan B, II* already in Alaska with sons Jon and Ross. All boats belong to the Whitney Fidalgo Seaport Company, headquartered in Seattle.

Left at the dock was the remainder of the family, wife Winona, daughter Marea and three daughters-in-law with their young children. Usually they all dash to Deception Pass where the boats arrive four hours after leaving Everett, to wave a final farewell for the two-month period. But this day they went their separate ways. The daughters-in-law had to get to their jobs. Once again, Marea would celebrate her birthday without father and brothers. Although having just graduated from college, she had not once had her father home for her birthday.

The time away from home is not always pleasant for John and his crew, either. They face rough seas, fog and other dangers. Mr. Borovina vividly recalls his 1963 trip. He was skipper of the *Cypress* and was accompanied by friend Willis Calvin, skipper of the *Martle,* a similar boat out of Anacortes. They were in heavy fog and were following a radar-equipped lead boat. (Today almost all fishing boats have radar.) They lost visual contact and both were grounded on rocks where they sat high and dry for two days waiting for an exceptionally high tide.

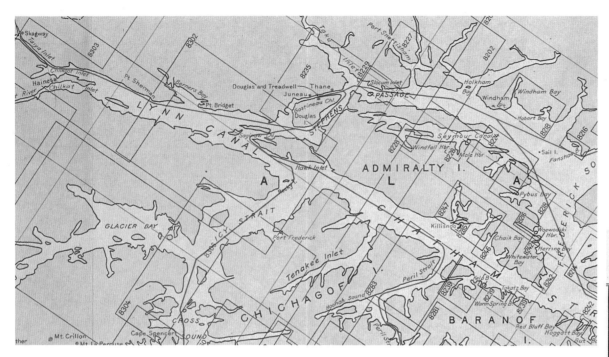

M.S. *Blowed in.* .... VOY ......

SAILING FROM .... TO ......

DAILY CONSUMPTION			PROGRESS	
ITEM	ON HAND NOON	USED	MILES BY ENGINE	
FUEL OIL			MILES IN STILL WATER	
LUB. OIL			MILES MADE GOOD	
FRESH WATER			AVERAGE KNOTS	

ADDED ITEMS	12:00 M.N. TO 4:00 A.M.	4:00 A.M. TO 8:00 A.M.	8:00 A.M. TO 12:00 N.	12:00 N. TO 4:00 P.M.	4:00 P.M. TO 8:00 P.M.	8:00 P.M. TO 12:00 M.N.
ding	0°	780°F		800°F		
EMP		178°F	Fishing	180°F		
sure		44 lbs		44 lbs		
RED. GEAR		225		220		

ADJUSTMENTS - INSPECTIONS - EMERGENCY MEASURES & REMARKS

Start Engine 05:29
Fresh water pipes frozen — withdraw
Left harbor 06:30
Lubed shaft & engine cyps 06:45
Fished for 4 Hour & had to
run in to Lazy Bay. Blowing
like hell!

Mrs. Borovina is terrified of such dangers and decreed years ago that no more than two of her sons be allowed on any one vessel.

The boats leaving Everett were late for the season's opening. Just three days earlier the Alaska Fishing Commission announced its opening would be Sunday. It was already late Monday afternoon. This was a coup, John thought, designed to give special advantage to Alaska-owned vessels. It would take the *Star of the Sea* five days, running 24 hours a day, to reach the fishing grounds. John would be allowed to fish 27 of the 61 days spent in Alaskan waters.

The typical fishing day off Alaska, John says, begins about 3:00 a.m. After a quick cup of coffee and toast, the net is set. On a good day the purse seine is set and emptied about 12 times. Lunch and dinner are between the setting of the net and its retrieval.

About 11:00 in the evening the cargo is transferred into the tender ship. Loaded to its capacity it takes four hours to empty. By then it is almost 3:00 in the morning and time for a new fishing day.

After returning from Alaska John reported, "This is the best fishing season I have ever had. Salmon have been on the increase for about the last five years. I think the reason is the fall-off of foreign fishing immediately off our coasts. This is the biggest year for everyone since 1949. Unfortunately the price is way too low."

According to custom, the catch profits are divided into tenths. Each crew member, including the skipper, gets one-tenth, and the other four-tenths are allocated to boat and net. The skipper gets a share of that. Crew members are charged against fuel for the vessel, food and other common costs.

A good Alaskan fishing season is critical for survival. Although salmon fishing generally opens in Puget Sound waters from September through November, it is overrun with fishermen, many from Alaska. The general pattern in the Sound is for seiners to fish during daylight hours and the gill-netters to fish by night.

During the Sound's fall season, restrictions are tight; fishing is allowed only one or two days a week. Indian fishermen have entirely different restrictions and are allowed to fish many more days than non-Indians. After his return from Alaska, John would fish for salmon off the San Juan Islands,

Edmonds and especially in Hood Canal. Says John, "I couldn't possibly survive if limited to fishing in Puget Sound."

Until three years ago, Mr. Borovina and sons fished for cod and sole by drag net trawling during winter months, but such bottomfishing has become increasingly difficult. "I don't think it's worth the effort anymore," says John.

During May and June of each year, John spends most of his work day dockside at the Port of Everett. In small garage-like, rented spaces, nets are repaired and various maintenance chores are tended.

Despite the good year, John worries that a dynasty of fishing for the Borovinas may be coming to an end. "When my father and I started, it was a good time. We looked forward to the fishing season. There were fewer regulations then, and the fishing was good. Fishing really gets in your blood. But over the last 10 years things have changed—too many restrictions, not enough fishing days. It used to be that we only had to worry about catching the fish; now we have to worry about regulations. It's getting harder for the younger generation to get into the industry and make a good living."

Another problem in gaining entry is difficulty in acquiring a license. Even sufficient money is not always enough as no new licenses are being issued. They must either be purchased from someone or inherited. Moreover, each license is only for particular waters in Alaska—Bristol Bay, the Kodiak area or southeastern Alaska. The Bristol Bay license now costs well over $100,000 and one for southeastern Alaska about $50,000. Today's profit potentials simply do not warrant such a large initial outlay.

John spent the winter of '85-'86 enjoying the sun in Yuma, Arizona. He is hoping for another good year.

Puget Sound salmon at Pike Place. John Alwin photo

Gillnetting is the most widely used form of commercial salmon fishing. Craft range from almost rowboat size to boats 40 feet or more in length. Nets are paid-out from a large power reel six or more feet in diameter (the diameter is regulated for different waters). The reel is located either on the stern (sternpicker) or the bow (bowpicker) of the boat. Mesh size of nets is regulated and varies from about five to seven inches, depending on regulations and type of salmon sought. A net is approximately 1,800 feet long and 65 feet deep. The top, as with the seine net, is held on the surface of the water by floats; the bottom is weighted down by a lead line. Each gillnetter has several nets, costing about $7,000 apiece. If the fisherman is lucky, a net may last 10 years. Once a salmon gets its head in the mesh, its body cannot pass through and is caught by the gills, hence the name gill-net.

Salmon also are caught from small boats, called trollers, on troll lines attached to the boat by pulleys. On the lines are sub-lines hooked and baited with herring. This method is time-consuming and rarely as effective as netting methods, but numerous small boats in the salmon industry are rigged in this manner.

In contrast to commercial methods of catching salmon, the sports fisherman must fish with only one rod and line using barbless hooks. The common method is by mooching, keeping the boat stationary, or trolling by moving the boat slowly for-

Clockwise from upper left: Indian gillnetter, Eddie Sherman, prepares his net at Seattle's Shilshole Bay. John Alwin photo   Even if fishing is not the most lucrative business these days, at least it is a picturesque one. John Alwin photo   Although some bays have been closed due to water pollution, southern Puget Sound, especially Hood Canal, remains prime oyster country. Here, worker picks oysters at Tarboo Bay, Hood Canal. Joel W. Rogers photo   Racks dangling shells are floated out over an oyster bed during spawning season to provide attachment surfaces for spats (newborn). John Alwin photo

Sunset at Poulsbo. John Alwin photo

ward. For deep bottomfish the sports fisherman may employ a downrigger, a heavy weight of lead attached to a wire cable to carry hook and bait to the bottom.

Today the most common method for catching bottomfish is by using large nets trawled along the bottom. This method is used for cod, rockfish, sole, hake and other species of bottom feeders. Trawl gear is heavy, making sizable boats a prerequisite. Longlining is another method used to catch halibut and cod. In this case, however, the line is about a half mile long, anchored and buoyed at each end, with shorter lines and baited hooks tied to the main lines. The larger boats carry several longlines, called skate, which are set out one day and hauled in the next.

Crab boats, really ships costing several million dollars each, also operate out of Puget Sound. They crab the Alaskan waters during the summer season and are refitted with trawling nets to catch hake and other bottomfish off the Washington coast during the winter season. Crab pots, weighing hundreds of pounds each, are baited traps that rest on the ocean floor. The large crab vessels, called catcher processors, are piled high with crab pots on the way to and from Alaska, looking like miniature container ships. They have cleaning, filleting and freezing facilities on board.

Despite the diversity of methods used, salmon are perhaps the easiest fish in the world to catch, and therein lies the problem. The easiest ways are illegal, meaning more time and effort must be spent than otherwise would be necessary.

At about age four, Pacific salmon leave saltwater to enter freshwater rivers and streams to spawn just before dying. Historically they arrived in great hordes, such that some small streams were almost solid with these fish during runs. All Indians had to do to catch them was set up a simple net or spear them, both now illegal methods.

Such an abundance of salmon caused early fishermen to think of the resource as inexhaustible. By the 1880s fish traps, with their system of funneled nets, were set on wood pilings at most of the strategic fish passes in the Sound. As would be expected, big canning companies came to dominate the industry. At the canneries, which were in almost every community, low-paid Chinese labor cut, cleaned and packed the salmon.

Because of the large number of salmon in the early years, anyone in a rowboat could make a living catching the fish. Many new immigrants, especially Slavs, Greeks and Norwegians, came to depend on fishing for a livelihood. As technology improved, they caught more fish and there were more small-scale fishermen. In 1910 masts and beams were added to aid in pulling in gillnets. With the development of the gasoline engine, which eliminated the muscle-straining nine-foot oars, people in small boats could fish widely in the Sound.

Large canning plants had almost a monopoly on fish traps, a method that annoyed other commercial fishermen and, especially, sports fishermen. That the traps were effective was undeniable. As recently as the Twenties, fish traps took a majority of salmon, including more than 80 percent of the large, prime chinooks, or kings. At the time, of the more than 200 traps on the Sound, well over half were controlled by just nine canning companies. Independent fishermen and the sporting public began working together to outlaw the traps.

In 1934 Initiative 77, which banned fish traps, passed by a wide margin. (The initiative also outlawed purse seiners from the Southern Sound, but they were reinstated in 1972). With fish traps outlawed, all persons again presumably had an equal opportunity to catch salmon. Regardless, the same consequence was inevitable—there soon would be more fishermen and boats than could support a living for those in the industry. Simply put, there would be too many fishermen chasing too few fish.

Below left: Chinese workers dry fish in West Seattle, 1906. Washington State Historical Society, Tacoma, WA photo   Below: Gig Harbor shipbuilding crew, circa 1926. Today those of Yugoslavian ancestry still account for the majority of fishing boats at Gig Harbor. Tacoma Public Library photo

Technology continued to improve. When new, lighter marine engines replaced the older ones, more hull space became available for fish. By the 1950s nylon nets, which did not rot and were stronger and more durable, replaced the old linen ones. The result was a gillnetter's dream.

Purse seine technology also increased dramatically and more boats were added. As recently as the early '50s, the typical purse seiner required 8 to 10 men to work the heavy nets. In 1954 a Yugoslavian immigrant invented a hydraulic powerblock for hauling in the heavy seine nets. Produced and marketed by MARCO (Marine Construction and Design Company) of Seattle, the powerblock almost instantly swept the industry. By 1960 every respectable seiner in the Sound had one. Crew size was reduced to three and the number of times a seiner could set its nets in a day tripled.

A walk along the colorful fishing docks at Seattle's Salmon Bay or at Tacoma, Everett, Gig Harbor, Poulsbo or any of the many home ports of the Sound's fishing fleet, may be a prerequisite to understanding this most traditional of Puget Sound pursuits. The sights, the sounds, the smells of the fishermen's world have been a part of the Sound for generations. For the photographically inclined, this is the stuff calendar photos are made of. Unpretentious commercial fishermen mending their nets or working on equipment dockside usually are happy to talk to passersby. In the last half of the Eighties many are disgruntled with an industry that has been mired in problems and have specific ideas on how best to manage the fisheries.

SALMON: AN UPDATE

For Puget Sound fish farmers like Domesea, the nation's largest producer of pen-raised salmon, life is relatively easy when compared to those who pursue the pens' free-swimming kin. Beyond the controlled pens of Sound fish farmers, the world of Northwest salmon fishing is an emotional and complex one involving hatchery and naturally spawned fish, Indians and non-Indians, commercial and sports fishermen, and several states, the federal government and Canada. Traditionally the industry has been mired in controversy, conflict, court cases, regulations and declining catches. Until very recently there seemed little reason for optimism.

Pacific salmon are anadromous, meaning they spend their adult life in the ocean and return to the freshwater of their natal rivers to spawn, either dying enroute or after spawning. These historically great salmon runs were key to the culture and subsistence of the Northwest's water-oriented Indian tribes. In the late 1800s, use of exploitative fish wheels and traps caused salmon stocks to plummet. Declines continued into this century as a consequence of loss of habitat, migration-blocking dams that put spawning grounds out of reach and more contemporary over-harvesting.

As the resource dwindled pressure on it grew. The situation reached a crisis point in the Sixties and Seventies. Based on their interpretation of the 1850s treaties by which they signed over their land to the United States, area Indians ignored state fishing restrictions. Fish-ins and even a shooting of one of the organizers along the Puyallup River made headlines. In 1974 U.S. District Court Judge George Boldt issued his landmark decision affirming Indians' rights to fish, as the treaties promised, at all "usual and accustomed stations." He decreed that

Indians had a right to catch half the salmon and steelhead taken from Puget Sound and off the coast. In that year Indians had only landed somewhere between 12 and 18 percent of the salmon harvest. In a subsequent decision, District Court Judge William Orrick ruled that treaty rights granted tribes included the protection of salmon habitat. Declining numbers exacerbated conflicts, for Indians half of a little was even less, and what remained had to satisfy the non-Indian commercial and sport fishery and still leave enough to replenish numbers. Clearly more was needed than mere court decisions divvying up rights.

Three recent developments are sufficient for some long-term optimism. The 1980 passage of the Northwest Power Act was a giant step forward in efforts to enhance the region's salmon fishery. Finally, after more than a half century, the federal government decreed that the Columbia and Snake rivers be managed equally for both power and fish and that efforts commence to undo decades of damage to the Northwest's fishery. The Columbia once was the greatest salmon producer on the continent, but dam building had devastated that important function and the title has passed to British Columbia's Fraser River. Until now fishing has taken a decidedly back seat to power generation. Fish ladders had been constructed on many of the dams, but still half the Basin's spawning area remained beyond reach of salmon. Likewise, little attention had been paid to the plight of the juvenile salmon trying to descend rivers to the ocean—many are lost to dam turbine blades. With a projected cost of about $800 million, this will be the biggest wildlife/fish enhancement program in world history.

On the Washington front, peace between the state and tribes was achieved in 1983. On March 3 and 4, at what is now known

as the Port Ludlow Salmon Summit, parties worked out allocations. In years prior to the peace conference the state was engaged in litigation with the tribes on an average of 75 times per year. During the next 3½ years the state went to court only three times with the tribes for a total of about 15 minutes.

Peace between the state and tribes and even the massive federal effort to resurrect the Columbia Basin salmon "factory" would not have been sufficient to bring Northwest salmon back from the brink. Salmon respect no state or international borders and range widely between their spawning and feeding grounds. After dodging dams down the Columbia to the ocean, a chinook salmon may migrate thousands of miles to Gulf of Alaska feeding grounds. Enroute and in those waters it may be caught, or what fisheries people call intercepted, before it has a chance to return home to spawn. Likewise, migrating Canadian fish are liable for interception by American fishermen. Thus even monumental gains in the Columbia Basin salmon propagation potentially could be fished away beyond Washington and even United States jurisdiction.

The need for a U.S.:Canadian salmon treaty has been talked of for years, but it was not until 1985 that the U.S.-Canada Interception Treaty became law. It called for an immediate roll-back of salmon harvests off Alaska and British Columbia and set the goal of allowing the state or country that spawned the salmon to benefit from its investment. As a result, more salmon will return to Washington waters, eventually making a larger harvest possible for all.

It took decades of abuse to nearly destroy Northwest salmon—the Pacific Salmon Committtee hopes to rebuild stocks by 1998. Initial dividends to sometimes impatient sport and commercial fishermen already are apparent.

In echelon purse seiners at Gig Harbor, one of the most authentic of the Sound's traditional fishing communities. John Alwin photo

The Mighty Military

Pugetopolis is replete with military installations. All kinds of activities, ranging from simple training bases to sophisticated high-tech testing facilities, ordnance depots, fueling stations, air bases, a Naval shipyard, an underseas warfare station and a nuclear submarine base circumscribe the Sound. The Army, Air Force and Navy, as well as the Coast Guard and the National Guard are all well represented.

Possibly no other urban area in the United States contains such a sizable assemblage of defense activities. Prominent are Fort Lewis, McChord Air Force Base, the Puget Sound Naval Shipyard, the Trident Submarine Base and the Naval Undersea Warfare Engineering Station. Economically the Tacoma and Bremerton areas are dominated by the military and Everett, with its anticipated Navy base, soon may be. Among the larger communities only Seattle and Bellevue remain somewhat free of military dominance.

The might of the military becomes even more evident when defense-related contractors are included. Among the largest are The Boeing Company, Todd Shipyards, Marco Shipyards, Tacoma Boatbuilding, Lockheed, Honeywell and Vitro.

Unlike in frontier days when populations near military installations felt more secure than those more distant, the nuclear and space age has created an opposite awareness. Pugetopolis has a sizable assortment of peace promoters and antinuclear groups whose followers are less than thrilled with the military-industrial complex and the consequent ground zero status for their area.

U.S.S. Long Beach, *a guided missile cruiser, and the world's first nuclear powered surface warship, at Bremerton's Puget Sound Naval Shipyard. Official U.S. Navy photo by Lance Skidmore*

With a dearth of commercial ship construction Todd Shipyards on Seattle's Duwamish River relies heavily on government contracts. Ronald Boyce photo

Target Seattle and similar peace groups would have preferred to live in a "Lesser Seattle" if a large and growing "Greater Seattle" only can be achieved by making the area a prime military target. On the other hand, some in Tacoma and Bremerton are providing a counterforce to the antinuclear advocates. To them the security of their jobs is crucial to their survival.

The military's significance in Puget Sound is one of its most prominent cultural features. Employment at just the region's largest half dozen installations exceeds 60,000. All totaled, military employment in 1986 approximated Boeing's 79,000 Seattle-area employment the same year. In addition there are more than 40,000 retired military in the Tacoma and Bremerton areas alone. Many others reside in and around Seattle. When military families are included, perhaps 400,000 people directly depend on the military coffers.

FORT LEWIS

In terms of both area and population, Fort Lewis is the giant among Puget Sound military installations. Outsiders wonder why and how Fort Lewis became one of a handful of the nation's key Army bases. Other places had loftier beginnings, more amenable climates and perhaps superior strategic locations. Moreover, at the time Fort Lewis (then called Camp Lewis) was established, Washington had little Congressional clout. Locally Seattle already had Fort Lawton. The answer is: the people of Tacoma actively sought the facility and got it!

By 1900 the U.S. Army had decided to abandon most of its earlier forts, sell them and concentrate its operations in eight division-size centers strategically located in non-urban areas. Army officers testifying before Congress in 1902 stated that the purpose in building new posts was "to get the Army posts out of the cities and large towns, and establish them upon larger tracts of cheaper land

in the neighborhood of the same cities and towns so that the men have the benefit of the country air instead of city air, and more room for training and exercises; the neighborhood of the barracks may be under military control; the rum shops and brothels may be pushed farther away from the men . . ."

In 1916 when the Army investigated possible sites for a major military post in the region, the Nisqually Plain south of Tacoma was not on the official list of candidates. Residents of the City of Destiny had other plans. Tacomans were adamant that they had the perfect site to accommodate a major Army base to serve this corner of the continent. The Nisqually Plain-American Lake area was relatively flat, well-drained and was sufficiently distant from the vices of big-city Tacoma so as to prove attractive to the Army.

Tacomans mounted a well planned campaign. First the people of Pierce County voted seven to one in favor of issuing a multi-million dollar bond to purchase a 70,000-acre site to be donated to the

Army. Their timing was perfect. The Army needed money and the offer of free land, just months before World War I, made the deal all the more attractive. Fort Lewis became the first military installation in the United States to be created directly as the result of an outright gift by citizens.

With the declaration of war things happened quickly, and the first buildings were finished within three days. In fact the Army moved on site before all details of land transfer had been finalized. Within three months, 1,757 buildings were erected and 422 of the structures were ready for occupancy. The camp began receiving soldiers. Almost overnight 60,000 men moved in and began training at Camp Lewis, the largest military cantonment in the United States.

However, when the war ended, the Army began to lose interest in making Camp Lewis one of the great Army posts in America. By 1923 even some military personnel began referring to it as a ghost post. The wooden buildings were not maintained

93

and quickly deteriorated as the number of on-base soldiers diminished to fewer than a thousand. Tacomans were furious and claimed the Army had reneged on the gift agreement. For wisely tacked onto the original land transfer was the stipulation that "if the United States should ever cease to maintain such tract as site for a permanent mobilization . . . title to the land so donated to the United States will revert to the County of Pierce, State of Washington."

Tacomans demanded their land back. The Army stalled. In June 1925 the Pierce County Commissioners, by vote of the citizens, were instructed to begin proceedings to reclaim the site. The Army then tore down over 800 buildings and sold them for scrap. Those in Pierce County were peeved. For months almost nightly fires destroyed or damaged 250 buildings. The camp was ringed with guards, but the fires continued and no suspect was ever found. In 1926 the Secretary of War, having decided not to abandon the post, asked Congress for funds to rebuild Camp Lewis with permanent structures.

After reclassification as Fort Lewis, now a full-fledged Army post, the wartime cantonment was transformed into a permanent installation. Streets were laid out in idyllic Garden City style. The entire encampment was modeled in accordance with the City Beautiful movement. There were traffic circles, tree-lined boulevards, underground wiring and assorted parks. The fort was designed to resemble a New England town, complete with ivy-covered brick buildings, creating an architectural atmosphere alien to that of the Pacific Northwest. Even today the Georgian architecture and strange street patterns elicit double-takes from visitors.

There are more than 25,000 military and 5,800 civilians employed at Fort Lewis. Another 1,500 military and 800 civilians work at nearby Madigan Army Hospital. The community of Lakewood is the unofficial residential area for off-base Fort

Left: Maintenance and repairs on the huge transports are full-time work at McChord Air Force Base. Below: Two of McChord's two-squadron fleet of giant C-141 Starlifters. Joel W. Rogers photos

Lewis personnel. Here also, builders adopted an architecture foreign to the Northwest with the early business center of Lakewood decked out entirely in New England colonial style. With its more than 30,000 retired military (including 19,000 Army and 11,000 Air Force) and thousands more active personnel, the Lakewood district may have one of the highest concentrations of patriotic Americans in the country.

Fort Lewis is the home of I Corps and the 9th Infantry Division, which accounts for 16,000 of the post's 25,000 soldiers. Among other nondivisional units are the 2/75th Ranger Battalion, which is trained to conduct commando operations in any environment, and 1st Special Forces Group, reactivated in 1984. The base's 135 square miles provide a variety of environments for training—dense forests (two-thirds of the fort area is timbered), plains, rugged topography, lakes and coastal settings. Fort Lewis also operates the 400-plus-square-mile Yakima Firing Center outside Yakima in eastern Washington. In contrast to lush Fort Lewis, the sub-installation provides a dry, desert-like setting and is well suited to support Mid-East training requirements.

Expansive Fort Lewis is a city in itself. It has almost 5,000 buildings including 3,500 family units, a shopping mall and other stores and shops, 5 elementary schools, 3 libraries, 5 theaters, a museum, hospital, taxi service, numerous recreation facilities, a weekly newspaper, 28 miles of rail and hundreds of miles of paved roads.

McCHORD AIR FORCE BASE

McChord Air Force Base, like neighboring Fort Lewis, constitutes another coup by the citizens of Tacoma and Pierce County. McChord is located on the former Tacoma-Pierce County Airport site (it was begun in the late Thirties as an Army airfield using WPA funds). Like Fort Lewis, the land was donated by the local government. Since its inception McChord has continued to grow. Today the 4,500-acre installation, with its 5,700 military and 2,000 civilian personnel, is a major Air Force base.

McChord began as a bomber base with its first aircraft B-18s and B-23s. During World War II it was the nation's largest bomber training base, with the famous B-25 Mitchell bomber the number-one aircraft.

In 1950 McChord became home to the North American Air Defense (NORAD) Command's 25th Air Defense Squadron. It is the primary base responsible for air defense of the northwestern part of the United States. The actual job falls to the 318th Fighter Interceptor Squadron with its McDonnell Douglas F-15 Eagles, some of which are on constant alert.

McChord is also home of the 62nd Military Airlift Wing. It provides airlift of troops, cargo, military equipment and passengers using two squadrons of giant C-141 Starlifters and one squadron of smaller C-130 Hercules aircraft. The base also serves as an aerial port of embarkation for Alaska and the Far East.

95

THE BOEING COMPANY

Within three questions, the average newcomer to Seattle invariably asks the one question no native can answer satisfactorily: "Where is Boeing?" The visitor expects to be shown precisely the Boeing plant. However anyone who has lived in Seattle-Tacoma for more than a month knows that Boeing is almost omnipresent. It is impossible to point to any specific building and proclaim, "there is Boeing."

Boeing is seemingly everywhere, its more than dozen major facilities scattered about metro Seattle, in Everett, Bellevue, Kent, Renton, Auburn, Tukwila and other areas. One place there is no evidence of Boeing is where everyone most expects to see it, in downtown Seattle. There is no downtown "Boeing Building," no skyscraper bearing the company's logo, no counterpart to Chicago's Sears Tower or Detroit's General Motors Building. Instead, The Boeing Company is spread all over the map.

Even when one finds a Boeing plant, only occasionally can its nature and purpose be deciphered. Many of its activities are top secret, making the content and purpose of some plants mysterious. Every parking lot is guarded by those who have memorized the "Sorry, but you can't park here," line. Entering one of the buildings is virtually impossible without prior approval.

The Renton plant produces fourteen 737s every month. Here a 737-300 is rolled out late at night. Boeing Commercial Airplane Company photo

At Paine Field near Everett, 747s and 767s are produced at the main assembly building, which covers 62 acres and, by volume, is the world's largest. Boeing Commercial Airplane Company photo

But Boeing is much bigger than its cavernous plants. By almost any yardstick, it is impressive. It is the Northwest's largest company. In 1986 the aviation giant employed 79,000 of its 112,000 workers in the Seattle area. Economists calculate that each job in a plant generates 2.5 jobs in the region. Locally it is a sizable "university," providing classes for almost 5,000 students in such fields as computer science, engineering and management. In the Seattle-Tacoma area Boeing, as an educational institution, is exceeded in size only by the University of Washington and Bellevue Community College.

The Boeing Company is made up of a series of operating companies—the Boeing Commercial Airplane Company and Boeing Military Airplane Company the largest two. Boeing is a leader, not only in commercial jetliners and military aircraft, but in missiles, rockets, helicopters, hydrofoils/jetfoils, spacecraft and in electronic and computer fields. Even so, the company keeps such a low profile that most Sounders are unable to name its president.

Boeing is not restricted to metro Seattle. The company also has major facilities in Wichita, Philadelphia, Dallas, Huntsville, Portland and, with the 1986 purchase of de Havilland Aircraft, in Toronto, Canada. The Boeing Company's primary headquarters is located in the city of Seattle, but all area production facilities are outside the city in suburban locations.

Boeing began in 1916 on the shores of Lake Union as the Pacific Aero Products Company. It soon moved into the famous Red Barn, now part of the Museum of Flight. There, William Boeing, from a well-to-do timber family, and Conrad Westervelt, a Navy officer and engineer, teamed up to build two piano wire-spruce-linen fabric "B and W" biplanes. Incorporated in 1917 as the Boeing Airplane Company, the name was changed to The Boeing Company in 1961.

From its inception, Boeing and the military have been close partners. During World War I the Red Barn plant built Model C trainers and a few flying patrol boats. With the end of the war, aircraft production almost stopped and the new concern had to shift to manufacture of sea-sleds and even bedroom furniture. Some C-700 seaplane and B-1 flying boat production kept the aircraft part of the business going, but this was a slack time for the fledgling company. Perseverance paid off in 1921 when Boeing received its first major post-war airplane order—to modify 111 observation planes. Other large orders followed and the decision

Right: Wartime production of B-29s   Below: Fearful of Japanese aerial attack, the company camouflaged its critical plant, smoothing the edges and creating what from the air appeared to be a hilltop residential area replete with streets, houses and even model cars. The Boeing Company Archives photos

to remain in the aircraft business was vindicated. By 1928 the 800 employees made Boeing one of the nation's largest aircraft plants. Boeing was here to stay.

When the United States entered World War II, Boeing's B-17, the Flying Fortress, was the nation's primary aerial striking force. The company's Seattle plant shifted entirely to bomber production and, the month following the attack on Pearl Harbor, was producing B-17s at the rate of 60 per month. That figure climbed to 250 per month in 1943. Deliveries peaked in March 1944 when 362 of the heavy bombers were built.

Despite its admirable speed, range and bomb payload, even the B-17 did not have the range or striking power for the vast Pacific theater. An even more impressive plane was required. Boeing engineers rose to the occasion with the B-29 Superfortress in 1942, the plane that would carry the war to the Japanese mainland. By war's end, the company had produced 6,981 B-17s and 2,766 B-29s. Following the war Boeing shifted to jet bombers, first the six-jet B-47 Stratojet in the late Forties and the first models of the B-52 in the early Fifties. Production of the durable B-52 stopped in 1962, but the latest G and H models are expected to remain in service through this century.

In 1952 Boeing announced that it was developing a commercial jet airliner and, two years later, relying on its swept-wing B-47 and B-52 military aircraft as models, the 707 prototype was born at the Renton plant. From this prototype the 727, the 737 and in 1970 the famous 747 followed. An entirely new plant to accommodate this giant commercial superjet was built at Everett. Appropriately, the world's largest jet airliner would be assembled in the world's largest building.

In the 1960s, Boeing did well, not as a result of military airplane construction, but

The Giant 747, the world's largest airliner at Seattle's Boeing Field. Boeing Commercial Airplane Company photo

because its venture into building commercial aircraft proved to be a supreme success. In early 1968 employment peaked at 149,000. Pre-production orders for the 747 were piling up and the company soon would be under contract to develop the Supersonic transport, the SST. Everyone expected the boom to continue. As a confirmation of confidence in the future, Seattleites chose "Supersonics" as the name for their new professional basketball team.

Then everything that could go wrong, did. Demand for the 747 faded fast and a great glut of unsold planes stacked up around the perimeter of the new Everett plant. The company's airplane orders dropped to 91 in 1971, down from 412 just six years earlier. In 1971 the government terminated the SST program. As a consequence, Boeing slimmed down, with employment plummeting from almost 150,000 in 1968 to a low of 53,300 in October 1971. Unemployment in the Seattle area soared. An optimist came to be defined in Seattle as anyone who still worked at Boeing and took a lunch, the expectation being that a pink slip would not be delivered before noon. Laid-off employees began displaying doomsday bumper stickers. Some even rented a billboard with the message, "Will the last one leaving the city, please turn out the lights?"

Actually, many of the unemployed refused to leave. Seattle's amenities were just too appealing. Instead the newly unemployed took any job they could find. Some formed new companies, often highly technical and successful. In doing so, they helped create a

more diversified regional economy. The Boeing bust cured the one-airplane-company-town image of Seattle.

Following another recessionary decline in the early Eighties, Boeing now is back in financial good health. Company employment again tops 100,000 in 1986 with the lion's share in the Seattle area. With a mix of military and commercial orders and greater diversification in the areas of software, computers, robotics and electronics, the company hopes to avoid the jolting highs and lows that have been the norm. Large orders for planes still make headlines in the *Times* and *P-I*, but the fact that Boeing's Computer Services is the company's fastest growing sector may be an early indicator of things to come.

PUGET SOUND NAVAL SHIPYARD

Visually and economically the Puget Sound Naval Shipyard dominates Bremerton, even more than Fort Lewis and McChord A.F.B. do Tacoma. Bremerton, population 36,000, is a Navy town and proud of it.

For generations, in both times of peace and war, hundreds of thousands of sailors have spent time at Bremerton while their ships were repaired, overhauled or while awaiting the commissioning of a newly constructed vessel. For many the time spent at Bremerton was their introduction to the Puget Sound area. Many liked what they saw and have returned to make the area their permanent home.

Puget Sound Naval Shipyard was established in 1891 as a Naval Station, but it was not until later in the 1890s and the Spanish American War that it received recognition. Its involvement in the war was indirect when it finished the old battleship *Oregon* and sent it on its long voyage to a Naval engagement off Cuba, but that was enough to put the facility "on the map." With most repair of battle-damaged American ships in World War I done on the East Coast, the Bremerton yard concentrated on building new vessels. Major vessels completed included 25 sub-chasers, 6 submarines, 2 minesweepers and 7 sea-going tugs.

During World War II emphasis shifted from new ship construction to repair of battle damage to ships of our fleet and those of the Allies. It began with the repair and modernization of the five battleships that survived the Japanese attack on Pearl Harbor. With an active Pacific theater during the war, activity at Bremerton expanded rapidly.

Civilian employment at the yard peaked in 1945 when it totaled approximately 33,000. The Navy would have preferred a work force of 38,000 to 40,000 civilians, but the area lacked sufficient housing. Row upon row of temporary housing all over Kitsap County just wasn't enough to accommodate the requisite numbers of workers. At times 40,000 to 45,000 sailors also were in port awaiting repair of their ships.

The Korean conflict saw many mothballed World War II ships at the yard reactivated. More recently the mothballed battleships *Missouri* and *New Jer-*

Facing page: Temporary war time housing for workers at the Bremerton Yards was scattered throughout Kitsap County, connected to the Base by no less than 80 bus routes. Official U.S. Navy photo

Right: A play on words at a Bremerton eatery. John Alwin photo   Far right: Early 20th Century penny postcard. Courtesy of Bonnie Marsh   Below: Thirty to forty ships are still mothballed at the Bremerton Yards, including these three aircraft carriers. Ronald Boyce photo

Floating Crane, Puget Sound Navy Yards, Bremerton, Washington.

sey have left for modernization and reactivation. Only 30 to 40 ships remain in storage at Bremerton.

Today its expansive in-town facility yard with its seven piers, six drydocks (one is the second largest in the country) and hundreds of buildings make this the largest shipyard on the West Coast. Ships still are built, overhauled and repaired by the Yard's 11,000 civilian employees. In addition there are 1,500 military personnel, including the two 550-person crews for the home-ported *Camden* and *Sacramento*, two fast combat support ships used primarily with carrier battle groups. The number of sailors awaiting overhaul work can climb to 6,000, especially if that involves an aircraft carrier, but these are slow times at the yard. It is expected activity will pick up in the '90s when newer craft in the 600-fleet Navy come on line for repairs and maintenance.

NAVAL SUBMARINE BASE BANGOR

The second largest employer in Kitsap County and, for some, the most controversial, is Naval Submarine Base Bangor. It was selected as the first homeport of the TRIDENT submarine in

Refit Delta Pier, the largest single facility at the Bangor Base, can accommodate three TRIDENT submarines at one time (one in dry dock). Official U.S. Navy photo

The U.S.S. Ohio inside the Magnetic Silencing Facility. Official U.S. Navy photo

1973, winning out over more than 80 other sites. Factors working in Bangor's favor included: 1) the Navy wanted initial deployment to be in the Pacific; 2) the Navy already owned the 7,000-acre site; 3) quick access to the ocean via deep waters of Hood Canal, the northern Sound and the Strait of Juan de Fuca; and 4) availability of air cover from nearby McChord A.F.B. and Whidbey Island Naval Air Station in times of war.

Construction began in 1974 and the base became operational in 1981. It now employs 5,000 military and 5,000 civilian workers. In late 1986 six TRIDENT submarines (including the *U.S.S. Henry M. Jackson*) operated out of the base with another two anticipated by 1988. The Navy's most potent weapon, each carries 24 missiles and each missile has eight independent warheads capable of hitting targets over 4,000 miles distant. Submarines are served by two alternating crews, a Blue crew and a Gold crew. A submarine is at sea and submerged for 70 days before returning to Bangor for

25 days of refitting and checking before returning to sea duty with a new crew.

The base provides all necessary support facilities for the submarines and crews. The refit delta can accommodate three of the craft at once. Periodically each submarine must visit the Magnetic Silencing Facility. By travelling the world's oceans the metallic submarines pick up a magnetic signature. At the silencing facility, which includes a 700-foot wooden pier, submarines enter a giant basket-like affair for electromagnetic treatment. Magnetic silencing involves electrically realigning magnetic particles of the sub to minimize its specific magnetic signature, reducing the possibility of detection, identification and vulnerability to magnetically detonated mines. On a secluded part of the base the Strategic Weapons Facility Pacific assembles, inspects and tests the TRIDENT missiles. More than 300 marines have primary responsibility for security at the Weapons Facility. Nuclear warheads, missile motors and other supplies

destined for the Weapons Facility are shipped to the base via now much publicized "white trains." Locally a Bangor based Ground Zero group schedules public protest to coincide with the passing of the trains.

Unlike many older bases, contemporary Bangor, by design, has been developed in a clustered pattern and almost 95 percent of the installation remains unbuilt. A compact Core Area contains housing, recreation facilities (library, theater, gym, swimming pool, etc.), Navy Exchange and commissary and the 1,000-student-capacity TRIDENT Training Facility where crews spend most of their work days when not at sea. Both developed and undeveloped areas are carefully managed for environmental quality. Waterfront structures, for example, were built far enough from shore to allow juvenile salmon to travel favored shallow-water migration routes. Forests, wildlife, fish, air and water all are carefully managed and closely monitored.

The natural environment that enables the Naval Undersea Warfare Engineering Station to conduct sophisticated tests is also an ideal one in which to live and work. Official U.S. Navy photo

1914 the Navy made a thorough investigation of coastal waters between Canada and Mexico seeking the most suitable site for testing torpedoes. So important was Keyport that families who had homesteaded were removed in the name of national defense. In 1915 the facility opened. Today at the highly secret station, torpedoes, mines and other underwater destructive devices are developed and tested.

NAVAL UNDERSEA WARFARE ENGINEERING STATION

Ten miles or so north of Bremerton at Keyport and the entrance to Liberty Bay is the Naval Undersea Warfare Engineering Station (earlier called the Naval Torpedo Station). Here are employed 3,600 persons, of which all but 300 are civilians.

The selection of Keyport for torpedo testing is a tribute to the waters of Puget Sound. From 1909 to

EVERETT AND THE NAVY

Until mid-1985 it appeared that Everett would be the exception to the military circling of the Sound. However in late August, after a search of the West Coast and then the Sound for a prime deepwater port, the Navy announced the selection of Everett, not Seattle's piers 90 and 91, as the site for the Aircraft Carrier Battle Group for the northern Pacific, pending authorization of funds. The establishment of this base would complete the Sound's circle of military operations.

The long-range economic impact on Everett and Snohomish County would be significant. According to the Environmental Impact Statement prepared for the Navy, it is expected that population should surge by 27,000. When fully operational, the battle group would include 13 ships, among them the nuclear powered carrier *Nimitz,* two guided missile cruisers, destroyers, frigates and mine countermeasure craft.

By the late '80s the base should employ up to 8,000 military personnel and an equal number of civilians. The anticipated facility would be a godsend to downtown Everett. As in Bremerton, it would be adjacent to the downtown area at the Port of Everett's Norton Terminal and the Western Gear property. The base would require construction of a new pier, improvement of existing ones and a 1,600-foot breakwater. Because of space constraints, several support facilities would be located in Seattle at the Navy's Sand Point installation.

With an increasing number of ships, fleet dispersal and the changing geopolitics and resultant potential loss of overseas bases in the western Pacific, the anticipated Everett facility would fit well with Naval planning.

The Recreational Lifestyle
A Photo Essay

As a major metropolitan complex, the Seattle-Tacoma area has endowments consistent with such a sizable population center—symphonies, theaters, museums, art galleries, professional sports teams, zoos and other cultural and recreational attributes. Some are nationally and even internationally renowned. Yet to perhaps a majority of residents, it is the almost unlimited access to outdoor recreation that ranks highest on their list of leisure-time options.

This is an outdoor recreationist's mecca, the nation's down-vest capital. Seattle is home to Recreational Equipment, Inc. (REI), the nation's largest consumer cooperative. Sportswear manufacturers Eddie Bauer and Pacific Trail, both Seattle institutions, and others have made the city the nation's sportswear and outdoorwear fashion center.

"Weighing anchor" in sail boat or power boat, kayak or canoe to explore the water world of the Sound, heading off for a weekend wilderness hike high in the Olympics or Cascades, loading the camper for a week in area forests or going after 20-pound chinook salmon in nearby waters are all part of Sounders' prized recreational lifestyle. A myriad of outdoor options is available. In Rand McNally's *Places Rated Almanac,* Seattle and Tacoma are among just 17 of the nation's 329 metro areas to receive the highest possible score for outdoor recreation assets.

The following photo essay shows a sampling of the outdoor-oriented lifestyle that has been part of the Puget Sound for generations.

Estimates run as high as one boat for every eight Puget Sound residents. So basic is recreational boating in the area, some people buy time-shares in pleasure craft. John Alwin photo

Right: Recreating in area forests is a generations-old tradition. A 1912 caravan of auto stages carries visitors in their Sunday best through Mt. Rainier National Park.   Below: Auto camping Teens-style in the lake country just southwest of Tacoma. Washington State Historical Society, Tacoma, WA photos

Clockwise from far left: Urban kayaking in Elliott Bay, a silent encounter. Joel W. Rogers photo   Seattle pleasure craft at the ready, a scene that is repeated throughout the Sound. John Alwin photo   Although an interruption, a passage through the Chittenden Locks is a predictably amicable experience, and watching the procedure is a popular spectator sport. John Alwin photo   Each spring, Opening Day festivities signal the start of the new boating season. Joel W. Rogers photo   For many, the Recreational Lifestyle is maximized when fully equipped. Norma Boyce photo

Clockwise from far left, facing page: Houseboats in Portage Bay opposite the U of W campus. Residents can and do step off their front deck into their boat and head off to a Husky football game or a waterfront restaurant. John Alwin photo   Countless Sound families have photo albums that include snapshots like this one of Jim Nelson, with the "small" chinook salmon he caught from the Green River, literally in his backyard. Photo courtesy of George and Belva Nelson   Time out at the Seattle Center. John Alwin photo The Sound to Narrows Run, a Tacoma tradition. Jonathan Nesvig photo   "Doing the Puyallup" (going to the Western Washington Fair) and filling up on onion burgers go hand in hand. John Alwin photo   Seattle's Kingdome is a truly multipurpose facility accommodating professional sports teams, home, boat and auto shows, even the famous Boeing Company Christmas party of 1980, claimed to be a world record for the largest party ever held. John Alwin photo

Nestled between the Olympics and the Cascades, Sounders are able to "get away from it all" and escape to a mountain world with a minimum of time and effort. Right: En route to Boston Glacier, Mt. Buckner in the North Cascades. Joel W. Rogers photo Far right: For Seattleites day or night skiing at Snoqualmie Pass is within an hour's drive. John Alwin photo Below: To the west the lush Olympics are a favorite retreat for area recreationists. Joel W. Rogers photo

Joel W. Rogers photo

The Photographers

Most of the contemporary photos in this volume were taken by:

Joel W. Rogers, *a professional Seattle-based photographer who centers his work on people and the out-of-doors and has a special affinity for the marine environment of his hometown. His photos are in demand and appear regularly in Northwest regional magazines, as well as national outdoor and environmental publications. His address is 1907 First Avenue, Seattle, WA 98101*

Jonathan Nesvig, *Assistant City Editor for Tacoma's* News-Tribune. *He also is an accomplished photographer with a special interest in travel-related and scenic subjects. He regularly contributes photos to regional publications. His address is 2915 N. 27th Street, Tacoma, WA 98407*

John Alwin, *editor and publisher of the NORTHWEST GEOGRAPHER Series. In the process of delving into each of the Series book topics, he has a chance to exercise his ability to artfully capture distinctly geographic subjects. He can make a glacial erratic (a big rock) look like fine art.*

NORTHWEST GEOGRAPHER™ Series

No. 1

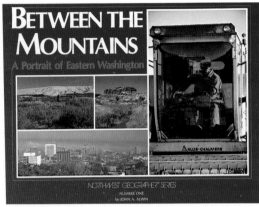

BETWEEN THE MOUNTAINS: A Portrait of Eastern Washington, by John A. Alwin
ISBN-0-9613787-0-0

In *BETWEEN THE MOUNTAINS,* geographer John Alwin takes you through Washington's big, open country east of the Cascades and introduces you to the land and residents of this unique and too-often stereotyped region. Already a classic, the 128-page book includes almost 250 pictures in brilliant NORTHWEST GEOGRAPHER™ color, two dozen historic photos, maps and an easy-reading, non-technical 50,000-word text.

> "an excellent profile . . . clear readable prose and first-rate color photography."
> WASHINGTON MAGAZINE

> "Fascinating text is enhanced by 248 color photos . . . the book promises great things for the Series."
> *Seattle Times-P.I.*

> "an informative and affectionate overview of the region and its people." *Spokesman-Review*

> "slick, lavishly illustrated . . . an informational showcase of Eastern Washington written by a still-curious expert in the field."
> *Yakima Herald-Republic*

No. 2

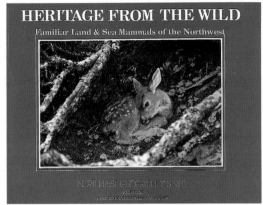

HERITAGE FROM THE WILD, by Douglas and Suvi Scott
ISBN 0-9613787-1-9

In *HERITAGE FROM THE WILD,* Douglas and Suvi Scott showcase more than 50 land and sea mammals of Washington, Oregon, Idaho and western Montana. This unique book places animals from the entertaining red squirrel to the behemoth gray whale in their geographic, historic and human context. Included in the 116-page volume are 150 stunning color pictures by some of the Northwest's finest wildlife photographers, full-color pictures of prized Audubon lithographs and an informative 50,000-word text.

> "beautiful photographs make it a delight to look at, informative, well-balanced text makes it a pleasure to read." WASHINGTON WILDLIFE

> "a valued addition to the library of anyone who loves the Northwest and its magnificent animal life." *The News-Tribune*
> Tacoma, WA

> "gorgeous . . . sensitive." *The Oregonian*

> "beautifully illustrated, informative book."
> OREGON COAST MAGAZINE

Next in the Series, No. 4
COASTAL OREGON
by Richard L. Price

The NORTHWEST GEOGRAPHER's tradition of excellence continues with *COASTAL OREGON.* Coast native and geographer Richard Price wrote this volume as a labor of love, and it shows! Sensitive, perceptive, complete, and all in a delightful writing style. *COASTAL OREGON* is destined to be an award-winner.

A volume with a difference. All the beautiful photos you've come to expect from an Oregon Coast book and much more. Understand the place where nature never stops. Walk the beaches, explore the shifting sands and marvel at the variety of coastal life. Come to know the Indians and early explorers. Meet today's fishermen, farmers, lumbermen, retirees. Discover the mosaic that is Coastal Oregon.

Don't miss a single volume! To complete your collection, or to be added to the Northwest Geographer Series mailing list and receive information on pre-publication discounts on forthcoming books, write:

Northwest Panorama Publishing, Inc.
NORTHWEST GEOGRAPHER™ Series
P.O. Box 1858
Bozeman, MT 59771